LIGHT FOR THE GENTILES

Paul and the Growing Church

WESTMINSTER GUIDES TO THE BIBLE

Edwin M. Good, General Editor

LIGHT
FOR
THE GENTILES

Paul and the Growing Church

by
LELAND JAMISON

Philadelphia
THE WESTMINSTER PRESS

Contents

Preface

WHEN the modern Protestant American Christian thinks of the church, he is apt to think of the organized congregation of which he is a member and of the softly lighted sanctuary in which he worships. But in the beginning there was little organization and there were no great houses of worship. How, then, have we come to where we are today? Or, an even better question: What is the nature and purpose of the church of our Lord Jesus Christ?

In this little book, Professor Jamison takes the reader back to the beginning. But this is no dry-as-dust textbook in ancient history. Here one walks with Paul the apostle and those men and women, named and unnamed, who were guided by the Holy Spirit in the turbulent days when the young church discovered what it was and what it was not. Here we see what these first Christians thought and did in the face of an all-powerful yet decaying government, a religious heritage that was their own yet not their own, and a bewildering array of religions that offered enticing answers to all problems. And here we see them coming to understand themselves as the people of God called to witness to the meaning of the life, death, and resurrection of Jesus Christ.

7

The Westminster Guides to the Bible grew in the first instance out of the stimulus of the Layman's Theological Library. If, we thought, laymen in the church could be so eloquently encouraged to be theologians, why could they not be encouraged to be Biblical scholars as well? In the modern resurgence of serious thinking about the Christian faith, Bible study has played a major role. But the methods and results of this recent study have not been made available to laymen.

The Westminster Guides to the Bible seek to fill this gap. In nine brief volumes, we introduce the riches of the major portions of the Bible and of the period " between the Testaments." The writers share the conviction that the Bible lies at the heart of Christianity, and that it is imperative that laymen be aided to take a firm grip on Biblical faith. We are certain that this means no denial of the mind. On the contrary, the Bible demands the utmost our minds can give it, and searching study repays our efforts with new insights.

Of course, we are primarily concerned with the Bible, not with our books about it. We hope that the reader will have his Bible in hand as he reads these books, and will turn to it again when he has finished. We dare to hope that he will turn from these guides to the Bible itself with greater anticipation.

And it is with laymen, who are the backbone of the church, that we are concerned. We have written, not for scholars already learned, but for those who seek to learn. We are certain that no wishy-washy faith, no cheap " religiousness," is wanted. In the vigor of Biblical faith we trust that the reader will find invigoration. If so, the church of Christ will be served.

EDWIN M. GOOD

CHAPTER 1 | *A Look Ahead*

FROM THE JORDAN TO ROME

THE enduringly significant events of the first century of the Common Era were almost totally ignored by contemporary historians. Suetonius, in his *Life of Claudius* (XXV), casually mentioned a disturbance among the Jews of Rome, which had been instigated by a certain " Christos." Tacitus (*Annals,* XV, 44) told how Nero, after the great fire of A.D. 64 in Rome, had sought to lay the blame on some self-acknowledged Christians, who were bitterly despised by the populace of the city. Pliny the Younger, writing to the emperor Trajan in about A.D. 110, described a curious group of persons in Bithynia who worshiped " Christ as a god." The Jewish apologist and historian, Josephus, toward the close of the first century related fragmentary stories about the work and fate of John the Baptist and about the death of James, commonly identified as the brother of Jesus. In short, the career of Jesus of Nazareth and the birth of the Christian community can be only vaguely documented in non-Christian writings of the period. All substantial information comes from writings produced within the community itself.

Nevertheless, nothing is more historically certain than the fact that during the years A.D. 30–100 there occurred certain events whose religious and historical significance can scarcely be measured. The Roman Empire collapsed in time, but the Christian church lives on and influences the life of mankind in the twentieth century more powerfully than ever before. And it is organically related to that unique cluster of events which are described only in those books which comprise the New Testament.

THE EARLIEST CHRISTIAN BOOKS

The most important books in the world, so Christians say, are the four Gospels of the New Testament. It is obvious why this is so, inasmuch as those four relatively brief books record the salient facts of the career of Jesus, selected and interpreted in the perspective of faith. Yet the Gospels do not and cannot stand alone. The work of Jesus did not end at Calvary or even in those strange experiences which are described in the stories of the resurrection. The " Christ-event," as it has been called, extends far beyond the boundaries of Jerusalem, far beyond the public acts and words of the historical person, Jesus of Nazareth. Just as the history of Israel, preserved in the Old Testament, is the indispensable prelude to the mission of Jesus, so all Christian history represents in a true sense the extension of God's unique and decisive saving action in Christ. The gospel history is not yet concluded, at least until that consummation of the history of salvation which the New Testament terms " the end." Therefore, the distinction between the several sections of the New Testament — or, for that matter, between " canonical " and " noncanonical " accounts of God's mighty works in human affairs — is of limited validity. All history, indeed, if we could read it rightly, reveals both the judgment and the mercy of God. The Bible, however, in both its major parts, gives testimony concerning the very special activity of God in the history of a particular people, and this testimony provides the essential clue to an understanding of his dealings with his entire creation.

Integral to the Gospels, then, are those other books of the New Testament, which tell about the emergence and growth of the church, the community of faith in Jesus Christ, during the first generations after he " suffered under Pontius Pilate." Traditionally, these are the books of the apostolic age, when the original disciples of Jesus still lived, continued his mission, and gave expression to their understanding of his saving significance. In the second and third centuries of the Christian Era, when the church was consolidating its structure and beliefs, it was generally assumed that all the New Testament books had been written by either apostles or intimate companions of apostles. The Gospels of Matthew and John were supposed to have come from apostles among the original Twelve, while Mark was reputed to have been a junior colleague of Peter, and Luke a fellow traveler with Paul. Accordingly, the criterion determining the acceptance of any particular book as a part of the extended Christian Bible was the *apostolic* affiliation of its presumed author. Modern scholars are by no means certain that all the New Testament authors can be so precisely identified. There is little doubt, however, that Paul wrote the majority of the letters that bear his name. It is generally agreed, further, that the other New Testament books, with a possible exception or two, were written within the lifetime of men who had personally known believers of the first Christian generation. Accordingly, readers may approach the New Testament with the confidence that virtually all its parts lead back into the very dawn of the faith in Christ, the period that remains somehow normative for all subsequent developments of Christian faith and life.

The letters of Paul are the earliest surviving writings of Christianity. The first Palestinian believers probably did not concern themselves with the writing of books or even tracts. Grasped by a wonderful new relationship with God, they were primarily eager to tell others about the good news, and it may be that they expected Jesus to return in triumph from heaven so soon that there was neither time nor necessity for writing about the origin of their faith. Jesus was remembered among them — what he did, what he said, how he had impressed those whom he confronted in Galilee and Judea. They also proclaimed the meaning of his life, death, resurrection, and exaltation, and the outline of this proclamation became the common possession of the early preachers. But, so far as can be discovered, no one *wrote* anything of importance until Paul began to correspond with his converts and fellow believers in the Gentile churches.

The chronological sequence in which Paul wrote his letters is a matter of great uncertainty. At an early date they were arranged according to length, and that order is followed in modern printed editions. Unfortunately, the chronological clues in the letters themselves are tantalizingly indefinite, so that scholars are forced to make more or less informed guesses about precise dating and order. Difficulty is increased by the circumstance that several of the letters — notably II Corinthians and Philippians — are each composed of two or more originally independent fragments. Another controverted point concerns the so-called "prison letters," Philippians, Colossians, Philemon, and Ephesians (if it is really Paul's): were they written from Ephesus, Caesarea, Rome, or some unknown place of imprisonment? It is generally agreed that the two letters to the Thessalonians are the earliest of the extant letters. In all likelihood, they were written sometime prior to A.D. 51. A fixed date in the career of Paul is suggested by Acts 18:12, which tells of Paul's trial at Corinth before the Roman governor, Gallio. Evidence from Roman history and inscriptions indicates that Gallio held this post in A.D. 51 or 52. If this is true, the remaining letters must have been written after A.D. 52 and thus mirror events of the last decade of Paul's work.

Another fixed point, although not datable to the year, was the great crisis of Paul's residence in the province of Asia, when he learned that Jewish propagandists were pressuring Gentile Christians in Galatia and Corinth to conform to Jewish ritualistic law. Some of the letters may be arranged according to their apparent relation to that crisis; that is, whether they seem to precede it, reflect its full bitterness, or look back upon it in retrospect. It must be admitted that no two scholars agree fully in their solutions of these problems. Nor is such agreement absolutely essential. What is required is the recognition that the letters illuminate various aspects and phases of Paul's work as missionary and pastor, chiefly during the last ten or twelve years of his activity, and that they open up the inner life of the Gentile churches to our sympathetic inspection.

THE FIRST CHURCH HISTORY

Invaluable as the letters of Paul surely are for throwing light into the many dark corners of the primitive church, by themselves they offer only an obscure and partial glimpse of the church's total development. Happily, another writer, who had probably accompanied Paul in his later journeys, composed the first " history of the Christian church" within approximately two decades after the death of Paul. This two-volume work, which we know as the Gospel of Luke and The Acts of the Apostles, carried the story of the " Christ-event" from the angelic announcement of the coming birth of Jesus down to Paul's arrival at Rome to stand trial before the imperial court. That the same person wrote both these books is evident from the preface attached to each. A tradition of the late second century, doubtless based on earlier information, assumed that this person was Luke, a companion mentioned twice in Paul's letters as well as once in the pseudonymous II Timothy, a book that may contain genuine Pauline fragments.

In the manner of all Biblical historians, Luke selected from the mass of information that he possessed those episodes which best illustrated his own conception of the growth of Christianity. He was a historical artist, rather than a prosaic chronicler, a " prophetic " spokesman concerned to " justify the ways of God to man."

Both halves of Luke's great history are addressed to a certain " most excellent Theophilus." It is not known who this man was, whether a friendly Roman official or a Gentile Christian of the upper social class. Luke wrote in order that Theophilus might know " the truth concerning the things of which you have been informed," but it is likely that he was also aiming his words toward a much wider audience. In any case, he proposed to " compile a narrative of the things which have been accomplished among us," and throughout his two volumes he incorporated information drawn from " eyewitnesses and ministers of the word," in addition to his personal observations as a companion of Paul. What was his purpose in doing this? It is seldom safe to attempt to explain the motives of an ancient writer, yet several conjectures may be offered.

By the final third of the first century the church had become largely Gentile in membership, broadly diffused over an area stretching from Palestine across to Rome, perhaps as far as Gaul and Spain. Eyewitnesses of the crucial Christian events were no doubt growing fewer, and a man with historical sense would have thought it necessary to preserve a reliable account of those all-important occurrences. Beyond that, however, there seems to be an " apologetic " intention in Luke-Acts. Stated simply, the author sought to prove the right of the supposedly " new " movement to exist and expand in the Roman Empire.

A legal case had to be made, due to the fact that the Empire prohibited the spread of new religions, in the interest of political unity and order. Numerous religions of great antiquity were recognized by the Roman government as legal, and their adherents possessed definite rights and privileges. Judaism was such a *religio licita,* despite all the difficulties that periodically arose between Roman officials and Jews in Palestine, Egypt, the city of Rome, and elsewhere. Accordingly, Luke-Acts developed the theme that Christianity was the true Judaism and as such was entitled to favorable recognition by the Roman government. In Acts, particularly, the author repeatedly demonstrated that not only was Jesus the fulfillment of Hebrew prophecy, but that the great leaders of the early church, including Paul, were loyal to their Jewish heritage. Further, the community of believers in Jesus the Messiah represented the only authentic Judaism of a new divine order, so that Jews who rejected their Messiah were scarcely entitled longer to enjoy their accustomed immunities. Finally, Acts emphasized that on many occasions Roman authorities had acknowledged the validity of the Christian case, by refusing to punish Paul and other missionary preachers in Gentile cities.

This theme, however, was not simply an artful legal plea. It was supported by more profound theological considerations. Jesus and all that he had initiated, including the progress of the church from Jerusalem to the capital of the Empire, had not been mere accidents of human history. On the contrary, all had happened according to divine plan, and it was the Holy Spirit of God who directed and activated the course of events at every juncture. God, not man, controlled the spread of the church and its message. Thus, the strongest argument for Roman toleration of the church is that which was attributed to the judicious Pharisee Gamaliel: "If this plan or this undertaking is of men, it will fail; but if it is of God, you will not be able to overthrow them. You might even be found opposing God! " (Acts 5:38 f.).

It would be a mistake to think that Acts was simply a clever defense against persecution: it was also a positive testimony to the mighty acts of God through Christ and in the church, and a powerful resource for the universal evangelistic enterprise. Actually, the book had various themes and purposes relevant to the faith and life of the evolving church. Basic to all was the desire to prove from Scripture and historical experience that the faith in Jesus as Messiah and Lord was a *true* faith, and that the community constituted in that faith by the Spirit was the growing nucleus of an unsegregated redemption available to all men.

The Shadow of Rome

" In those days a decree went out from Caesar Augustus that all the world should be enrolled." (Luke 2:1.) This brief sentence fixes the approximate date of the birth of Jesus; it also indicates the historical and cultural background of the rise of Christianity. For the overarching circumstance of the first age of Christianity was the Roman domination of the Mediterranean world. Since the death of Alexander the Great (323 B.C.), the lands of the East had been racked by unending dynastic struggles and local wars. Meanwhile, in the third pre-Christian century, Rome began its irresistible climb to power in the West, and within two hundred years its sway embraced all the lands bordering the Mediterranean. For the people of Israel the decisive point of this conquest was reached when Pompey entered the Holy City in 63 B.C. But this was only a minor episode in the vast extension of Roman power, which by 27 B.C. had become so complete that Octavian (soon to become Augustus) closed the doors of the temple of Janus in Rome, signifying that the whole civilized world was at peace. In terms of political and social conditions, the period of the early Roman Empire was surely the "fullness of time" favorable to the growth of emerging Christianity. Universal peace brought freedom and safety in travel and commercial prosperity. It was possible for a Paul to move almost at will through the Empire, and the widespread use of the Greek language permitted the literate traveler to make himself understood wherever he went.

The new cosmopolitanism tended to weaken the securities and loyalties of older and more compact social orders. No longer did the source of political and economic power lie close at home — the governing decrees were issued from distant Rome, and human destiny seemed to depend too much on the whims of a remote emperor. Thus was produced a "lonely crowd" of psychologically, if not always geographically, displaced persons, characterized by what Gilbert Murray has called a "failure of nerve." The loss of personal and local responsibility, which resulted from being swallowed up in the complex vastness of the Empire, led to a sense of the futility of human endeavor. Some men became cynical and sought temporary satisfaction in moral license; more, perhaps, turned increasingly toward the inner life and the assurances of supernatural religion. Gentile pagans were by no means godless; on the contrary, they worshiped gods many and lords many, in quest of a spiritual salvation that would transcend the insecurity and frustration of the present world.

No single formula can describe the bewildering profusion of religions in the Empire. From unrecorded antiquity each local area and ethnic group had worshiped their own gods (without denying that others existed). The local character of ancient religion can be seen in the cults of the several Greek city-states, or in the people-centered religion of the Hebrews. These are examples of the situation that obtained everywhere in the ancient world, although forces of the universalization of religion had been at work at least from the beginning of the great empires in the Fertile Crescent. This tendency gained momentum after Alexander and reached a climax in the religious cosmopolitanism of the Roman Empire. The names of gods changed from place to place, but it was increasingly recognized that the same divine forces were at work across boundaries. More importantly, the blessings sought in all the religions were approximately the same: health, safety, and prosperity in this life, climaxed by some kind of immortality beyond — or even preceding! — physical death. While Rome encouraged the growth of a national cult, centering in the traditional gods borrowed from the Olympian pantheon of Greece, but with special veneration of the deified reigning emperor, most of the particular religions catered rather to individual needs. By means too varied to catalogue — sacrifices, rituals, esoteric initiations, prayer, superstitious charms, and so on — men tried to conscript supernatural power for immediate personal benefits and to escape the threat of nothingness which menaced the merely human at every turn. This, too, was a preparation for the good news of redemption in Christ.

One ancient religion alone resisted the syncretistic forces with remarkable integrity. That was the religion of the people of Israel. The resistance was not absolute even among them, since the majority of Jews were scattered throughout the Empire and beyond, subject to constant and subtle infiltration of pagan ideas and customs. Judaism, nevertheless, owned a hard core of authoritative written tradition, contained in their sacred Scriptures, which defined their faith with a precision unknown in other religions. Further, wherever a Jew might live, he could look toward a holy land still inhabited by his kinsmen, a temple in which the worship of Israel's God was jealously maintained in prescribed purity, and a succession of devoted scholars who guarded the revealed law against foreign contamination. In every important city of the Empire stood synagogues, which kept in constant touch with the center of Judaism in Jerusalem. Moreover, some six hundred years of oppression and dispersion had served to put iron into the Jewish character and to intensify their self-consciousness of being the chosen people of God.

In Judea and Galilee, however, the tension between Jew and Roman grew increasingly severe from 63 B.C. on. In keeping with its usual conciliatory policy, Rome attempted to rule Palestine indirectly through the Herodian family, of partly Jewish origin, but the experiment was not successful. The history of the period, described in minute detail by Josephus, is bafflingly confused, but one generalization is possible: more and more Palestinian Jews cared less and less for Roman domination, direct or indirect, and hostility toward the conqueror flared up in frequent revolt. From A.D. 6 to 66 Judea was governed by Roman procurators (except for brief periods, such as the reign of Herod Agrippa I, A.D. 41–44). The most notorious of these was Pontius Pilate. Some of the procurators tried to mollify Jewish passions; others were guilty of corruption and callous disregard of Jewish religious sensibilities; none could stem the rising tide of Jewish nationalism. The unrest reached its culmination in the revolt of A.D. 66, when partisans of the old Maccabean stamp rose in Galilee and lighted the torch of rebellion. The Jewish patriots were able to stave off complete defeat until A.D. 70, when Jerusalem fell and the Temple was destroyed by the Roman legions.

Thus perished the last Jewish state of any consequence until the formation of modern Israel in 1948. Judaism, the religion, was gradually reformulated, with the Torah at its heart, and became ever more exclusive against the menace of an un-friendly Gentile world. Meanwhile, the Biblical heritage found powerful new expression in the community of those who saw in Jesus the fulfillment of the purpose of the one God of the universe.

How It All Began

THE Acts of the Apostles begins where the Gospel of Luke ended, with the final resurrection appearance of Jesus, followed closely by his ascension into heaven. Here, as the previous volume in this series has suggested, we come upon the event that is the solid foundation of the Christian faith, yet which also poses difficulties of bewildering complexity. *That* the disciples were certain of Jesus' victory over death, and *that* their certainty brought with it a new kind of faith, cannot be doubted. *What* they actually experienced is a question of another order, involving profound historical, philosophical, and psychological considerations.

This much is evident: Luke in both his volumes assumed that the buried Jesus somehow came to life again, abandoned the tomb, appeared visibly to his disciples, and talked with them over a period of forty days (Acts 1:3), and finally withdrew his bodily presence from them by means of a vertical ascension through the clouds. The Gospels of Mark, Matthew, and John agree with this assumption of visible appearances, and most Christians ever since have visualized the resurrection in this manner. It should be remembered, however, that Paul — who laid greatest weight on the fact of the resurrection

21

(I Cor., ch. 15 and throughout his letters) — may have thought of the event in less " materialistic " terms. He asserted positively that Jesus had " appeared " to numerous disciples and, apparently in the same form, to himself. Yet Paul never mentioned the empty tomb, and he distinguished explicitly between the " physical " body that was buried and the " spiritual " body that was raised. For him the resurrection and the glorification or exaltation of Jesus to the immediate presence of God may have been one and the same event.

In any case, neither the actual occurrence nor the precise mode of the resurrection appearances can be proved by coercive demonstration. Historical investigation can assert that at least some of Jesus' disciples *believed* that he appeared alive to them, but only the experience of faith in him who rose can verify the disciples' claim. The birth and continued existence of the church may lend probability to the claim, as may also the passionate witness of Christian believers throughout the centuries, but probability is all. Absolute proof is not attainable, and argument is mostly futile. Christianity jealously guards the objective occurrence of the resurrection as being of one piece with the total revelation of God in history. In the Biblical view, salvation must result from God's action, not from man's discovery of abstract eternal truth. Yet an honest Christian faith admits that the resurrection transcends the normal categories of historical inquiry. The necessary thing here is to see what the resurrection *meant* to those who did believe in it, as that meaning is concretely set forth in The Acts of the Apostles and in the letters of Paul.

The prospectus of subsequent developments was stated in the words that Jesus addressed to his disciples at their final meeting: " You shall receive power when the Holy Spirit has come upon you; and you shall be my witnesses in Jerusalem and in all Judea and Samaria and to the end of the earth "

(Acts 1:8). It was precisely the purpose of Luke's second volume to describe this process in terms of the irresistible spread of the gospel. The letters of Paul offer intimate insight into the manner in which the Spirit-guided witnessing reached its symbolic destination at Rome. It has often been remarked that the title " The Acts of the Apostles " is something of a misnomer, inasmuch as only Peter and Paul figure with any degree of prominence in the narrative, and the complete career of neither is related. Instead, the book might better be styled " The Acts of the Holy Spirit," since, as Luke details the history of the next few decades, the growth of the church proceeded by the mysterious guidance of the Spirit rather than according to the calculated intention of the disciples. After the withdrawal of Jesus from the realm of the disciples' sense perception, they paused to re-form their ranks. A successor to the traitor Judas was chosen, in order to preserve the meaningful number of twelve in the apostolic circle. A little band of some one hundred and twenty persons devoted themselves to prayer and doubtless wondered about the direction of their master's further work.

On the day of the Jewish Festival of Pentecost a revolution occurred among the expectant followers of Jesus: " they were all filled with the Holy Spirit " (Acts 2:4). The picture drawn by Acts offers a vivid scene of heavenly winds roaring through the house and of tongues of flame settling upon the believers. Inspired by the Spirit, they began to speak in many languages, so that Jewish pilgrims from all parts of the world could understand what the disciples were saying. We cannot be certain that the incident as related by Acts is fully historical. The story contains definite echoes of a rabbinic tradition concerning the reception of the law by Moses on Mt. Sinai, the event that later Judaism celebrated in the Feast of Pentecost. According to the tradition, God's words were miraculously translated into all the languages of mankind. Moreover, the Gospel of John reports that the Spirit was bestowed by Jesus on the disciples on the day of the resurrection, and both the Johannine and the Pauline conceptions of the Holy Spirit seem to be rather less spectacular and mechanical than the presentation in Acts. Nevertheless, the author of Acts intended to say that the Holy Spirit was given in an unmistakable manner at a definite time, and that this new gift brought understanding and inner power to the disciples, forming them into a distinctive community. The wind and fire and ecstatic speaking may seem quite fantastic to a modern reader, but the meaning of the story should not be ignored on that account. It points to the Holy Spirit, received by Jesus from the Father and poured forth upon the disciples, as the dynamic force in the life of the church. As John Knox has explained, " The church was born of the Spirit, and that Spirit was from the beginning recognized to be the presence and power of the living Jesus."

The Faith Is Proclaimed

Of greater importance than any unusual phenomena was the preaching of a sermon by Peter, and the beginning of that proclamation of salvation through Jesus which was to reach to the ends of the earth. This speech (ch. 2:14-40) is the first of a series recorded in Acts; several attributed to Peter (chs. 3:12-26; 4:8-12; 5:29-32; 10:34-43), one to Stephen (ch. 7:2-53), a few to Paul (chs. 13:16-41; 14:15-17; 17:22-31), in all of which the meaning of Jesus for salvation was interpreted. It is not to be supposed that Luke possessed complete transcriptions of such speeches, and it seems probable that he followed the model of Greek writers who often composed speeches appropriate to the known opinions of historical characters. Writing many years after the events described, Luke doubtless used traditional memories of what had been spoken on particular occasions, but he also presented these materials in the form of his own understanding of the Christian message.

From the beginning, however, Christian preaching apparently followed closely a common tradition about Jesus, as Paul suggests in I Cor. 15:3 ff.: "For I delivered to you as of first importance what I also received, that Christ died for our sins in accordance with the scriptures, that he was buried, that he was raised on the third day in accordance with the scriptures, and that he appeared to Cephas." Although each preacher added something of his own thinking to the basic outline, such an outline is discernible in the speeches of Acts, and it is corroborated in the letters of Paul and other New Testament writings. This basic proclamation is commonly referred to as the "kerygma" (a transliteration of a Greek word meaning "a public proclamation"). The kerygma was the essential Christian message, the form in which the church expressed its central convictions concerning the religious meaning of Jesus.

Behind the apostolic preaching lay, of course, the Old Testament, post-Biblical Judaism, and especially the message that Jesus himself had proclaimed. All of this cannot be adequately summarized in a few sentences, yet the thrust of previous expectations can be stated: The God of Israel, who had rescued his people out of bondage in Egypt, who had formed them into a nation and given them the Torah and a land of their own, and who had preserved them in good times and bad through the centuries, this same God had also promised, through his prophets, to give Israel a final deliverance and to inaugurate a glorious new age. Jesus had come announcing the nearness of the Kingdom of God, indeed asserting that in his words, works, and his own person the Kingdom was already in some manner present. Peter and all the early preachers ringingly affirmed that God had now begun to make good on his promises. The fulfillment of God's purpose was embodied in Jesus, in his ministry, death, and resurrection. The resurrection has most forcefully demonstrated that Jesus is the Messiah — the Christ — the head of the new Israel, the maker of the new covenant between the true Israel and God. The activity of the Holy Spirit among the believers is the sign of the Messiah's present power and glory. The full consummation of the new age is at hand; the triumphant Messiah may return at any time to complete his work. The preachers, Acts tells us, challenged " all the house of Israel " to recognize that Jesus was the Messiah, and all were invited to " repent, and be baptized . . . in the name of Jesus Christ for the forgiveness of your sins; and you shall receive the gift of the Holy Spirit " (Acts 2:38).

Several points in the Acts presentation are noteworthy. First, the work of Jesus was described as *eschatological* in character. That is to say, his Messianic Kingdom was to involve an end (Greek *eschaton,* " end ") of the present corrupted historical order, although not by normal political means. In ways not clearly defined (other than in the startling manifestations of the Holy Spirit), God would restore his creation to its intended form. Here it should be recognized that the New Testament presents no single explanation of how the end will come to pass. Some portions, as the Revelation of John, paint lurid pictures of apocalyptic warfare between Christ and Satan; other views are more reserved and " spiritual," as the Gospel of John and perhaps Paul in his later period. Undoubtedly the early kerygma had apocalyptic overtones, but the speeches in Acts, at least, contribute few details of that sort. There is an urgency in the appeal, to be sure, as though the decision for the Messiah must be made soon or never, but the aspect of cosmic upheaval is not labored.

Again, the message was directed at the outset to Jews alone. The church, recalling the idea of a " righteous remnant " envisioned by Isaiah and other prophets, conceived itself to be the New Israel. Yet there was, apparently, no notion of a " new religion," sharply distinguished from the old worship of God. The Scriptures of the Old Testament remained the Bible of the believers, and they appealed to the ancient prophecies to demonstrate that what happened in connection with Jesus was organically related to God's comprehensive strategy of salvation. The message, nonetheless, implied that the Israel that was to share in God's victory over evil would consist only of those who accepted Jesus as Messiah. The believers knew themselves to belong to this redeemed community, an Israel " according to the Spirit " (as Paul later put it) within Israel " according to the flesh." Not the accident of Jewish birth, but repentance and faith in the Messiah were the requisites of membership in the new community. This understanding paved the way for the ultimate extension of the community to include Gentiles as well as Jews. Yet the universalist implication was not fully realized at first among Jewish believers. In the view of Acts, the Holy Spirit was yet to guide the community in the direction of its intended inclusiveness.

THE FAITH IS LIVED

The preaching of Peter brought results, and Acts tells of three thousand persons who joined the community of believers. Although that figure may be somewhat exaggerated, there can be no doubt that the group enjoyed a gratifying initial growth in Jerusalem. From the beginning of Acts through chapter 12 the story focuses on the life and fortunes of the Jerusalem church, its inner experiences and its external relations with the general Jewish community, and the spread of its message by gradual stages into Judea, Samaria, and finally into Gentile territory. Throughout Acts the Jerusalem church functions as a kind of Vatican, the chief center of authority for all Christians. It will be seen, however, that Paul subjected himself in only a limited measure to the Jerusalem leaders, although he had great affection and respect for them until the end of his active career. What was true of Paul must have been true of many other unnamed Christian workers among the Gentiles. After A.D. 62, when James the brother of the Lord was killed at the command of the high priest, the Jerusalem group lost all authority over the widely scattered and predominantly Gentile churches, other than the authority of sentimental regard for the place where the crucial events had occurred. During the Jewish revolt of A.D. 66–70 the little group of Judean Christians fled across the Jordan and survived for an indeterminable period as a sterile and mostly unrelated appendage to the growing Christian organism.

At the start, nevertheless, the Jerusalem church was *the* church, so far as Acts is concerned. No direct information about believers in Galilee is given, although other evidence tucked away in the New Testament suggests that many believers lived in Jesus' homeland. In Acts we read only of the tightly knit fellowship of disciples in Jerusalem, known variously to outsiders as "those of the Way" or "Nazarenes," while they thought of themselves as disciples, brothers, and even "saints." The emergence of such fellowships within Judaism was not unknown. Judaism was the religion of an entire people, and apart from the Temple hierarchy and the religio-civic Sanhedrin possessed no organized "church" in the later Christian sense of that word. Synagogues could be established anywhere, apparently at will, by any ten male Jews of the requisite age. Moreover, there were religious parties and brotherhoods, comparable to fraternal orders in the modern world, or even to political parties. The recent discoveries of manuscripts and monastic ruins along the western shore of the Dead Sea throw light on such a brotherhood of Jewish sectarians around the turn of the Christian era. The Qûmran community had a Messianic faith, expected a great deliverance, considered itself the nucleus of God's true and permanent Israel, and shared a common pattern of worship and life. While no direct connection between the Qûmran Essenes and the early church has yet been demonstrated, the two groups exhibit many comparable features and illustrate the pluralistic structure of Judaism before A.D. 70. Accordingly, the formation of the new community of Jesus the Messiah would not necessarily have attracted great attention, nor would it have automatically excluded its members from participation in the national worship. The disciples continued to attend the daily services in the Temple and retained the good will of their fellow countrymen.

Yet they were also distinctive, in their beliefs, worship, and manner of life. They believed that the Messiah had come and would come again, and they " devoted themselves to the apostles' teaching " about this central fact of faith and its implications. Further, they joined together in constant prayer (presumably for the speedy consummation of the Messiah's work) and in the breaking of bread. The latter action doubtless included the sharing of all meals, but it also had reference to the Last Supper of Jesus with his disciples — perhaps every meal was both a memorial of his death and an anticipation of the great Messianic banquet to be held when the Kingdom should come. Some of them, if not all, pooled their economic resources and lived off their capital, as it were. There was no compulsion about this sharing as the references to the gift made by Barnabas (Acts 4:36 f.) and the curious story of Ananias and Sapphira (ch. 5:1 ff.) show. No abstract theory of communism was involved: it was simply a case of mutual assistance for the benefit of the poor, and a conviction that in the new age accumulated wealth would be of no importance. Few other churches of the New Testament period seem to have shared possessions in such a complete manner, although the practice of generous charity was a chief characteristic of all early Christians. The peculiar custom of the Jerusalem group was dictated by local and temporary circumstances, perhaps chiefly by the intense feeling of unity in the Spirit and by a fervent expectation of an imminent end to the existing world order.

It was a worshiping and waiting community; it was also a courageously witnessing community: " And with great power the apostles gave their testimony to the resurrection of the Lord Jesus, and great grace was upon them all " (Acts 4:33). This preaching brought a steady stream of new believers; it also excited the hostility of Jewish authorities. Acts records at least four incidents in which leaders of the community were arrested in Jerusalem, and it is likely that these were only typical instances. Roman officials figure in none of these stories, indicating that the disciples engaged in no political action. The issue was between those who preached about Jesus and the Jewish leadership which had caused his death. Ultimately the very validity of Judaism was at stake. If Jesus was the Messiah, then it had been a horrible crime to execute him, and the Judaism that rejected the Messiah was a perverted Judaism. Peter and the other preachers made precisely such charges and thereby came to the attention of the ruling clique. There followed a series of harassments, which flared up on occasion into genuine " persecution." Peter and John fared not too badly, it appears, inasmuch as they suffered only temporary imprisonment and were, indeed, aided to escape by divine intervention (Acts 5:19 and 12:7 ff.). A really serious crisis arose in connection with Stephen, who proposed a more radical interpretation of the new faith than had been ventured by the more orthodox apostles.

AN EVENTFUL SEPARATION

Stephen demands particular explanation, inasmuch as he represents a division within the community of believers. Acts intimates that starting with the great Pentecostal revival new disciples were drawn from among Greek-speaking Jews who were temporarily resident in Jerusalem. These were known as the Hellenists, a term which seems to refer to the linguistic and cultural background of certain Jews, rather than to Greek Gentiles. In any event, a dispute arose between the " Hebrews " or Aramaic-speaking, native Palestinian Jewish disciples, and those of Hellenistic origin. The reported point at issue was the unfair treatment of the Hellenist widows in the daily distribution of food. Acts 6:1 ff. relates that seven of the Hellenists were appointed to act as quartermasters for the entire community, so that the apostles might spend all their time in preaching. The story bristles with difficulties, and it seems probable that Acts has glossed over a more fundamental difference. Certainly the so-called " deacons " were immediately found to be preaching to other Hellenistic Jews. Stephen got into trouble when he proclaimed Jesus in a synagogue composed of men from outside Palestine. His presentation of the message seems to have struck the supposedly more " liberal " Hellenistic Jews as being subversive of all that they cherished. So it appears from the charge laid against Stephen: " This man never ceases to speak words against this holy place and the law; for we have heard him say that this Jesus of Nazareth will destroy this place, and will change the customs which Moses delivered to us " (Acts 6:13 f.).

If Stephen did speak in this manner, he was indeed a threat to the unity of Judaism. By his insistence that Jesus and the dawning new age made Torah and Temple obsolete, he cut a clear line of separation between the Messianic community and traditional Judaism. The older disciples did not recognize this principle of division so clearly, but the future development of the church lay along the path broken by Stephen. Perhaps already in Jerusalem he and his Hellenistic colleagues began to address the message to non-Jews; certainly preaching to Gentiles was the positive result of the scattering of the Hellenists after the death (an execution or a lynching?) of Stephen. It is significant that Peter and his close associates did not have to leave Jerusalem at that time. Even so, in the speech of defense attributed to Stephen (Acts, ch. 7), the latter argued still within the framework of Judaism. He appealed to history to prove that the Jewish majority had never given God the spiritual worship and moral obedience that He demanded; they had not observed the real *intention* of the law. By implication he asserted that the rejection of Jesus was the culmination of disobedience. It is evident, further, that Stephen presented Jesus as the center around which a truly obedient Israel would be re-created.

The martyrdom of Stephen precipitated events of fateful significance for the future development of the church. Some of the disciples were compelled to leave Jerusalem as refugees, and these initiated, quite gradually and unintentionally, the missionary thrust that was to make the church a truly universal institution. This universality was already implicit in the church's unique message of salvation, but the recognition of that universality was surely speeded by the crisis of persecution. Three verses in Acts summarize a chain of events which is not spelled out in detail but which nevertheless was determinative of the course that the mission would subsequently follow: " And on that day a great persecution arose against the church in Jerusalem; and they were all scattered throughout the region of Judea and Samaria, *except the apostles.*" (Acts 8:1; italics ours.) " Now those who were scattered because of the persecution that arose over Stephen traveled as far as Phoenicia and Cyprus and Antioch, speaking the word to none except Jews. But there were some of them, men of Cyprus and Cyrene, who on coming to Antioch *spoke to the Greeks also,* preaching the Lord Jesus." (Acts 11:19-20; italics ours.) Behind this terse statement lay the enthusiastic efforts of numerous and nameless witnesses of the faith in Jesus. Not by calculated design, we may conjecture, but out of the exuberance of passionate conviction, they broke through the crust of nationalistic exclusiveness and proclaimed the possibility of salvation to all who would hear and believe. And it was first at Syrian Antioch that the believers received the distinguishing and enduring name " Christians." (Acts 11:26.) It matters not that the word may first have been a derisive epithet; it positively served the purpose of identifying those who acknowledged Jesus as the Messianic agent of God's redemption.

It should be noted that although Acts relates that " they were *all* scattered," the apostles are excepted. At first glance this strikes us as curious: if a general persecution of the disciples was in progress, why should the leaders be ignored? Here it is necessary to recall that a division existed within the Christian community itself — Hebrews and Hellenists. We have suggested that this split went deeper than the matter of food distribution; almost certainly it reflected divergent understandings of the relation of Jesus to traditional Judaism. While we cannot confidently reconstruct the details of Hellenist beliefs, this much seems evident: they viewed the appearance of the Messiah as somehow making obsolete the hallowed observances of historical Judaism, perhaps even nullifying the authority of the Law as the norm of Jewish life and worship.

The author of Acts nowhere made the cause and legal ground of the persecution entirely clear, but we can fairly imagine that the Hellenists were branded as subversives, much as loyal Americans regard agitators who seek to overthrow the

Constitution by force. The so-called "Hebrew" disciples, on the other hand, apparently saw no necessity of modifying their inherited ways in religion, other than to prepare themselves ever more rigorously for the climactic return of the Messiah Jesus. It was no crime among the Jews to believe that this or that individual was the promised Messiah. Therefore, the Hebrew disciples could continue unmolested as an eccentric sect, as long as they made no frontal attack on the irreducible fundamentals of Judaism, such as the unity of God, the election of Israel, and the authority of the Law. The fact that an indigenous church survived in Jerusalem until after A.D. 66 attests that a certain kind of faith in Jesus was not wholly incompatible with the dominant pattern of Judaism. To be sure, at widely separated intervals James the son of Zebedee and James the Lord's brother were executed, but the grounds of condemnation were probably as much political as theological.

Acts offers several typical illustrations of the manner in which the good news was gradually offered to Gentiles. As the story goes, the transition was almost imperceptible, affecting first several types of persons who stood on the fringes of the Jewish community. Thus, Philip the Hellenist made his way into Samaria and was eagerly welcomed by many there. The Samaritans proudly claimed descent from the tribes of the Kingdom of Israel, which had fallen to the Assyrians in 721 B.C. Actually, their ethnic ties with the Jewish people were tenuous, and their religion represented a curious blending of the Pentateuch with non-Jewish elements. Nevertheless, their reverence for the law of Moses and their expectation of a Messiah provided points of contact for Philip's preaching. Acts is careful to show that Philip did not work as a free agent: his converts had to be "confirmed" by Peter and John, and the gift of the Holy Spirit came to Samaritan believers only after the apostles had placed their hands upon them.

The Samaritans were distant if disreputable cousins of the Jews, so that a mission among them did not constitute a total denationalizing of the new faith. Indeed, Jesus himself had traveled in Samaria and had won the allegiance of an errant woman. The next stages of the mission, however, brought a more serious strain on the kinship with Judaism. When Philip encountered an Ethiopian slave who was puzzling over the meaning of Isaiah, ch. 53, he convinced the inquirer that the prophecy pointed directly to Jesus. Moreover, Philip baptized the eunuch, thus receiving him into the number of disciples. This was surely a revolutionary advance beyond anything anticipated by the Jerusalem church, especially since on account of his mutilation the eunuch was not eligible to become a Jewish proselyte. But because the Ethiopian believed the truth about Jesus, Philip administered the rite of initiation into the people of the Messiah, without regard to the technical requirements of Old Testament law. In a similar manner Peter, in response to a God-inspired dream, went to the home of a Roman centurion in Caesarea and found ready acceptance of his message. This story is related at length in Acts, chs. 10 and 11, with the joyful conclusion that " to the Gentiles also God has granted repentance unto life."

The modern reader should approach these stories with a degree of caution and not be misled by the apparent simplicity and ease of the movement of the church beyond the boundaries of Judaism. On the one hand, it is certain that such a movement did take place quite early. Paul was not the first to preach to Gentiles; that honor belongs to the Hellenists, those Jewish believers who were at home in Greco-Roman culture and who refused to be chained by legalistic exclusiveness. They did not consider themselves other or less than Jewish — on the contrary, they were fiercely proud of their heritage of nation and religion, a heritage that Jews of the Dispersion often were able to preserve only by suffering and death. But they were able and willing to associate with Gentiles and to regard Gentiles as salvable, to a degree not common among Palestinian Jews.

This is not the place to consider the complexities of Hellenistic Judaism and its real, yet often quite subtle, differences from the religious thought and feeling of the homeland. The Hellenistic Jew had at least learned to live among and with Gentiles. And it was Hellenistic Jewish believers in Jesus who made the first advance to non-Jews with the gospel message. In this respect the case of Peter and Cornelius should not be regarded as an exception: the centurion was already a " Godfearer," which means that he subscribed to a great deal of Judaism, although he was reluctant to undergo the change of nationality which conversion to Judaism involved. Moreover, despite the attempt of Acts to assert that the Jerusalem church recognized Cornelius as a " brother " in the full sense, the subsequent controversies in which Paul became embroiled indicate that such recognition was never wholeheartedly granted to Gentile believers who had not become Jewish proselytes in the traditional manner.

CHAPTER 3

Persecutor and Apostle

Two Views of Paul

Aʟᴛʜᴏᴜɢʜ Luke did not intend to write a biography of any particular apostle, the figure standing out above all others in Acts is Saul of Tarsus, later known as Paul. Whereas in the first twelve chapters of the book the story concerns the fortunes of the Jerusalem church and its several leaders, with incidental references to the departure of the Hellenists, the second and larger part is devoted almost exclusively to Paul. He was the greatest representative of Hellenistic Christianity and the model of all missionaries. Moreover, the gospel that he preached was the true interpretation of the redemption in Jesus Christ.

Such was the conviction of the author of Acts, and he succeeded so well in his delineation of his hero that many readers unconsciously conclude that Paul was the *only* missionary who converted Gentiles in large numbers and organized them into churches, and that the Pauline statement of the meaning of Christ was unanimously accepted by all early Christians, including those of the mother church in Jerusalem. The fact, however, seems to be that Paul was only one, albeit the greatest, among *many* preachers of Christ who fanned out over the Mediterranean (and probably the Mesopotamian) world. Further, his own letters disclose that both his right to preach and the message that he preached were under constant attack by other Christians. The process by which the early church expanded as well as the portrait of Paul have been considerably idealized — and, one might add, stereotyped — by Luke. Both the historical development and the man were much more complicated than Acts discloses.

Nevertheless, Luke was essentially correct: as far as historical investigation can reach any firm conclusions about the first age of Christianity, it must declare that Paul did more to determine the direction of Christian development than did any other single individual. To say this is not to disparage the contributions of other faithful leaders: Peter, who was the first apostle to perceive the Messianic significance of Jesus (Mark 8:29), and to whom the risen Lord first appeared; or John, sometimes identified as the "beloved disciple," who stood bravely with Peter against opposition in the first days of the church; or the two Jameses, one the brother of John, the other "the Lord's brother." These and others, whose names have survived only in hazy tradition, proclaimed the basic message of salvation and gave basic shape to the life and worship of the primitive church. But in Acts, Peter and the others soon pass into obscurity, and Paul emerges as the chosen instrument of the Holy Spirit in the transmission of the gospel to the Gentiles.

Great as was Luke's veneration of the apostle to the Gentiles, it is necessary to approach his account with caution. Modern scholars have perceived that Luke was as much a theologian as a historian, concerned more about the revelatory meaning of events than about pedantic accuracy in regard to details of time, place, and occurrence. Consequently, in reconstructing the career and thought of Paul, the apostle's letters should be used as *primary* sources of reliable information, while the data of Acts should be considered as secondary, subject always to correction. Some matters are presented by Acts so differently from Paul's account that total harmonization seems impossible. Exhaustive studies of the historical discrepancies have been made, but these need not detain us here. It is well, however, to recognize in advance one aspect of real significance for the proper understanding of Paul: Acts pictures him as constantly subservient to the Jerusalem apostolate, reporting to it at regular intervals and tempering the radicality of his message in order not to offend the scruples of fellow believers in Judea.

The letters leave a somewhat different impression. In them only three visits to Jerusalem within his Christian period can be certainly identified. On one ("after three years," Gal. 1:18) he consulted only with Cephas (Peter?) and James the Lord's brother, being still not known by sight to other Christians in Judea; the second came "after fourteen years" (Gal. 2:1 ff.), and then Paul and Barnabas won from three apostles who "were reputed to be pillars" a presumably grudging approval of their Law-free gospel to uncircumcised Gentiles. The only concession to which Paul admits is that he agreed to "remember the poor." His third visit (promised but not described in the letters) was undertaken as a gesture of ecumenical reconciliation. By taking a large contribution from the Gentile churches of the Aegean area to the poverty-stricken believers in Jerusalem, Paul hoped to heal the breach between those who continued to insist on observance of the Law and those who embraced his message of justification by faith.

Acts is correct in its insistence that Paul never completely detached himself from the Jerusalem apostles; again and again his letters reflect his genuine respect and affection toward those who had been closest to Jesus and who were "in Christ" before him. His work, nevertheless, was carried on in almost total independence of them; he did not report to them after each journey; he defended his own apostolic credentials as being equal, if not superior, to theirs; he passionately argued that his understanding of the way of salvation in Christ was true, because he had received it from God and not from men. The sad truth seems to be — and even Acts has inadvertently left this impression — that his final mission of reconciliation failed. When he was arrested in Jerusalem, the leaders of the church there gave him no special help.

PROLOGUE TO CONVERSION

Sometime near the beginning of the first Christian century, in the Cilician city of Tarsus, there was born a Jewish boy who was destined to take his place among the authentic geniuses of all religious history. His name was Saul; his parentage is unknown, as are virtually all other details of his early life. Acts records that his family had somehow acquired Roman citizenship, a favor often granted to provincials who rendered some outstanding service to the Empire. We learn further from Acts (chiefly in the context of speeches supposedly delivered by Paul) that he studied the Law in Jerusalem under Gamaliel, a famous teacher of the first century; that he was a zealous member of the Pharisaic party, and that he was a tentmaker by trade. He is first introduced as an accomplice in the execution of Stephen, and subsequently as a ruthless persecutor of the new sect of believers in Jesus. These scanty bits of information are partly corroborated by the Christian Paul.

In his letters he boasts that he was a Jew with unimpeachable credentials: " circumcised on the eighth day, of the people of Israel, of the tribe of Benjamin, a Hebrew born of Hebrews; as to the law a Pharisee, as to zeal a persecutor of the church, as to righteousness under the law blameless " (Phil. 3:5-6); " I advanced in Judaism beyond many of my own age among my people, so extremely zealous was I for the traditions of my fathers" (Gal. 1:14). Concerning his birth and childhood in Tarsus, or his training with Gamaliel, Paul wrote nothing. His writings reflect intimate knowledge of Greco-Roman culture, at least in the measure that a piously self-conscious Jew of the Dispersion might be expected to be acquainted with the idioms, ideas, and values of pagan society. Indeed, if we were to read his letters apart from the testimony of Acts, we would have no notion that he had ever visited the Holy Land prior to his conversion. While it is not necessary, perhaps, to doubt that Paul first met Christian believers in Jerusalem, there remains a strong possibility that Damascus was the scene of that initial encounter. The place is not important. Wherever it was, the man who first sought to exterminate believers and later surrendered himself to their Lord was a loyal Jew, but a Jew wholly at home in the world of Gentiles.

That Paul did persecute Christians is beyond denial. Not so readily answered are such questions as: Which Christians? Why did he harass them? What punishments could legally have been inflicted on them? We have previously noted that only the Hellenistic Jewish believers were seriously molested in Jerusalem. In all probability Paul dircted his repressive activity against the same group, whether in Jerusalem or Damascus. A more difficult problem concerns the crime for which the believers were indicted. Inasmuch as wide differences of opinion and observance were tolerated within the Jewish community as a whole (the disciplines imposed upon themselves by the Pharisaic brotherhoods and Essene groups have no relevance here), it is certain that the persecuted Christians were suspected of attacking something absolutely essential to the integrity of the Jewish people and their faith.

This "something" must have been either the validity of the Law or the unity of God. Any assertion—by a person who claimed to stand *within* the people of Israel — that the Messiah Jesus had rendered the law obsolete and useless, or that this apparently human claimant to Messiahship possessed the attributes of God, would have stirred up charges of blasphemy. The latter was the most heinous of all religious crimes, punishable by death. It is altogether likely that both kinds of assertion were made by Hellenistic Christians. Small wonder that Paul, the fanatical, overscrupulous adherent of the Mosaic law, embarked on a campaign of extermination.

"HE . . . WAS PLEASED TO REVEAL HIS SON TO ME . . ."

Many miracles are recorded in Acts. But of all — lame men healed, the dead raised, prison gates opened — none was so unexpected, so dramatically demonstrative of the divine power and grace, so pregnant with future possibility, as the conversion of the Pharisee Saul. In a moment, without warning and contrary to his own desire, the fiery persecutor was transformed into a " slave of Jesus Christ." Three times Acts tells the thrilling story (chs. 9:3 ff.; 22:6 ff.; 26:12 ff.), with slight variations of detail between the three passages. But the main point — and the only point that the Pauline letters explicitly state — is plain: God "was pleased to reveal his Son to me." The relentless hunter of heretics was blinded by a heavenly light; he heard a voice which summoned him to follow a course exactly the reverse of his previous efforts.

Now he believed that the crucified Jesus was not a fraud and a disgrace to Israel, but rather the Messiah, the fulfillment of God's promises and of Israel's hopes. The consequences of spiritual revolution within a single man can hardly be measured. Paul (we shall use his chosen name) was not, as some hostile critics claim, the perverter of the " simple religion of Jesus," nor was he the " real founder " of Christianity. More than any other person known to us, he drew the line of separation between the faith in Christ and historical Judaism, between the Old Israel and the New; his ways of thinking about the meaning of Christ still determine the pattern of Christian orthodoxy. A *preserver* rather than a perverter of the essential gospel, Paul has again and again recalled the church from preoccupation with sterile human works to a fresh appreciation of God's gracious salvation in Jesus Christ. Surely by no method of reckoning was he " least of the apostles."

It would be fascinating but probably futile for us to speculate further on the whys and wherefores of the crucial change in Paul. It has been inferred from casual remarks in his letters that Paul was subject to a troublesome physical disorder, such as epilepsy or migraine headaches, and that this ailment may have rendered him susceptible to hallucinations. In other ways, also, recourse has been made to categories of abnormal psychology in order to explain his paradoxical conversion. We may not reject such explanations out of hand, but we should acknowledge that there is insufficient clinical evidence to permit an assured diagnosis. Two factors, however, do appear certain: Paul was a man of mystic temperament, and he probably was a Messianist before ever he became a Christian.

As Adolf Deissman has argued, Paul had a " mystical-prophetical nature," in the sense that he experienced communion with God and on occasion claimed to have received special revelations. The essence of religion to him was " immediacy of contact with the Deity." After his conversion he found this immediacy of contact exclusively through Christ, but there is no reason to doubt that always he had been predisposed toward that type of religious response. Moreover, although specific evidence is lacking, it seems overwhelmingly probable that he had long shared the common Jewish expectation of a coming Messiah. This expectation took no single, invariable form among ancient Jews, and we do not know what kind of Messiah Paul hoped for. Nevertheless, *any* idea of the Messiah would have made him a fair target for the revelation that he did receive. Having said so much, we must still concede that the New Testament attributes Paul's conversion purely and simply to a personal, unmediated confrontation by the exalted Christ. Did it happen so? To that question no scientifically coercive proof can be offered. As in the case of the resurrection of Jesus, we may feel that the historical results can only be accounted for by the cause that the New Testament describes, but other men of equal intelligence and honesty may feel quite the opposite. In accepting or rejecting we walk by faith, since the events were unique and cannot be repeated under controllable conditions. We can only "prove" that Paul believed it was Jesus who spoke to him, and that immediately Paul's whole conception of God's relation to man became focused on the one who so spoke.

Damascus and After

The sequel to the conversion bristles with historical problems, inasmuch as the primary and secondary sources appear quite in disagreement. In his letter to the Galatians — written some two decades later, and in defense of his divine commission to preach to Gentiles — Paul recalled the circumstances of his early Christian career in a few sentences: "I did not confer with flesh and blood, nor did I go up to Jerusalem . . . , but I went away into Arabia; and again I returned to Damascus. Then after three years I went up to Jerusalem to visit Cephas, and remained with him fifteen days. . . . Then I went into the regions of Syria and Cilicia. . . . Then after fourteen years I went up again to Jerusalem with Barnabas, taking Titus along with me." In this passage Paul maintained that his "ordination" as an apostle came directly from the Lord himself and depended on no human ratification.

He further claimed that he sought no personal contact with the Jerusalem church for at least three years after his conversion. He implied that his base of operations was in Damascus, but that most of the three-year period may have been spent in "Arabia." The latter term could designate vast stretches of territory lying to the east and southeast of Damascus, though we may infer that Paul remained in the more populous region of the Nabataean kingdom. His note in II Cor. 11:32 f. indicates that he had become somehow embroiled with the Nabataean authorities, since a representative of King Aretas of Nabataea tried to set up a road block around Damascus in order to prevent Paul's escape from that city. In a daring maneuver, the apostle hid in a basket and managed to pass through the guards outside the walls. The brush with Aretas was only the first in a long series of legal involvements stirred up by Paul's evangelical vehemence down to the end of his life.

The letters offer us no information about the "silent years" in Arabia, and Acts ignores the phase altogether. Imaginative commentators have pictured Paul as withdrawing from the world in monkish fashion, so that he might reflect on the full meaning of his soul-shaking experience, and then returning to civilization with a more or less full-blown theological system. This is highly unlikely. Paul may have been a mystic, but he was not a recluse. His favored milieu was the exciting atmosphere of great cities, in which he could proclaim his faith to masses of people. Doubtless he did in Arabia precisely what Acts tells us he did from the start: he preached about salvation through the Messiah Jesus to all who would listen, Jews and Gentiles alike. Nothing in his own direct testimony suggests that he ever restricted his message to Jews alone. The church with which he was first identified apparently practiced no segregation. In the early years, if he looked to any place as his headquarters, it was Damascus, not Jerusalem. Paul's home, we suspect, was where his hat was, and he was inhibited by no desire for ecclesiastical endorsement and supervision.

Luke, by contrast, sketches a rather different view of Paul's initiation into the missionary task and of his relation to the church of Jerusalem. As told in Acts, the blinded Paul was led into Damascus, to the home of Judas on Straight Street. Meanwhile, a disciple named Ananias was guided by a vision to seek out the notorious persecutor and to baptize him. In two accounts (Acts 9:15 and 26:16 ff.) of the event, the Lord revealed explicitly that Paul was to " carry my name before the Gentiles and kings and the sons of Israel." Elsewhere (ch. 22:21) this commission was given to Paul through a vision in Jerusalem. In any case, Paul began immediately to preach Jesus as the Messianic Son of God in Damascan synagogues, confounding the Jews by the force of his proofs. They plotted against him, and he barely eluded them by being let down over the city walls in a basket.

His next stop was in Jerusalem, where the authenticity of his conversion was doubted by fearful disciples, until the Cyprian Barnabas vouched for him. Thereupon Paul began to preach openly, particularly to Hellenistic Jews. Once again his assassination was plotted; again he was rescued, and the disciples took him to Caesarea on the Mediterranean coast. Thence he went back home to Tarsus, where he remained in obscurity for some time. Acts 9:31 turns temporarily from the chronicle of Paul with a curious remark: " So the church throughout all Judea and Galilee and Samaria had peace and was built up." If this verse is rightly placed (and it may not be so, since Acts was composed from several originally independent sources), it confirms our impression that two types of believers were active in Jerusalem, the one group mostly acceptable to their compatriots, the other regarded as dangerous to the survival of Israel and its faith.

Acts connects the significant beginning of Paul's missionary work with the founding of the church in Syrian Antioch. When the Jerusalem apostles heard that Greeks had been received into the fellowship by Hellenistic refugee preachers, Barnabas was dispatched to Antioch to investigate this unforeseen turn in affairs. He found evidence of the favor of God in the group and stayed on as a teacher. Soon he brought Paul from Tarsus to assist him. After a year of collaboration, the two were entrusted with a famine-relief contribution for the Christians of Judea. In Jerusalem the emissaries recruited John Mark, the cousin of Barnabas, to join them in their work in Antioch. Then came the fateful command of the Holy Spirit that moved the Antiochian church to appoint Barnabas, Paul, and John Mark to become missioners in other Gentile lands. The three embarked for Cyprus on the first of three major journeys attributed by Acts to Paul.

A comparison of this familiar narrative with the autobiographical remarks in Galatians leaves us in some confusion. Acts seems to tell both too much and not enough. The book gives no place to the secret " after three years " visit, which Paul intimates was the occasion of his first meeting with Cephas (Peter) and James the Lord's brother. Aside from those two apostles, he wrote, he remained " still not known by sight to the churches of Christian Judea." No such secrecy or anonymity characterizes the Lucan story at any point. Again, Acts has so compressed the course of events that it is difficult to account for the fourteen years in Syria and Cilicia mentioned in Galatians. On the other hand, Paul himself shows no recollection of visits to Jerusalem from either Damascus or Antioch, certainly not in the manner described in Acts. When we add to these differences the difficulty of identifying his " after fourteen years " visit with the Jerusalem conference of Acts, ch. 15, the question of just how closely he was related to the mother church becomes almost hopelessly baffling. Scholars continue to wrestle with this problem, but no firm consensus has been reached.

Out of the welter of apparently conflicting evidence we can emerge with a few reasonably assured generalizations: Paul, a Hellenistic Jew who may or may not have lived in Jerusalem, was converted, in or near Damascus, to a Hellenistic type of belief in Jesus; for many years — as few as eleven or as many as seventeen — he traveled as a missionary preacher of the good news, working in independence of the authority of the Jerusalem apostles; he greatly respected those apostles and, on one occasion fairly early in his career, went to Jerusalem to consult privately with Cephas and James; not until he had labored for a decade or so did he undertake an open meeting with the Jerusalem leaders; his letters suggest only one visit to Jerusalem thereafter, when he went to offer a collection, not from Antioch, but from all the churches of Asia Minor, Macedonia, and Greece. Such is the outline that seems to be reflected in his letters.

"To the Jew First . . ."

In one respect the Pauline letters and Acts fully agree: Paul was a man on the move. Neither the ivory tower of pedantic study nor the calm contemplation of a monastic retreat could contain his restlessness. No sooner had he recovered from the shock of the startling confrontation by the risen Lord than he began the driving search for new hearers of his destiny-determining gospel. Acts tells us almost nothing of his wanderings before Barnabas summoned him to Antioch, but from that point we find Paul seldom at rest. According to the conventional reading of Acts, he made three major journeys, exclusive of the final voyage to Rome as a prisoner. Whatever may have been in Luke's mind, Paul himself had no notion of three well-defined campaigns. He visited, it may be fairly assumed, many more places than those mentioned in Acts; his adventures were far more various and thrilling, by his own intimation in II Cor. 11:23-27. Nevertheless, we may trust the Lucan narrative for a general view of the areas that Paul penetrated, as well as of the strategies he used in carrying the good news to both Jews and Greeks.

At the outset, under authorization of the church of Antioch, Barnabas apparently took the lead as he and Paul, accompanied by John Mark, took ship to explore new fields. The campaign across Cyprus cannot be called spectacularly successful. Although no hostility from Cyprian Jews is recorded, neither are any conversions in the synagogues. Luke gives chief attention to an episode featuring the proconsul of the island and a Jewish magician attached to the governor's retinue. The Roman received the apostles courteously, but Elymas (or Bar-Jesus) bitterly attacked them, doubtless afraid that his influence over Sergius Paulus would be undermined. In a gesture reminiscent of Peter's dealing with Ananias and Sapphira (Acts 5:1ff.), Paul (in Acts 13:9 Saul is first called by his more familiar name) pronounced a curse of temporary blindness on the intruder. The tale concludes with the remark "the proconsul believed . . . for he was astonished at the teaching of the Lord." How much he believed is not told, and there is no claim that a church was gathered at Paphos. Paul later had other encounters with diviners and sorcerers, we may be sure, for practitioners of the magical arts preyed widely on the credulity of the ancients. The present story exhibits dramatically the superiority of the Christian apostles over all pagan pretenders to supernatural powers.

Beyond Cyprus, on the mainland of Asia Minor, the apostles found greater opportunity and success. After John Mark left them at Perga, Barnabas and Paul continued north and eastward through Pisidian Antioch, Iconium, Lystra, and Derbe. Although no paraphrase can improve on Luke's story, attention should be drawn to the *manner* of the mission, a manner characteristic of Paul's work throughout.

As might be expected, the apostles made their initial approach to fellow Jews in the synagogues of each city. Jews were as widely scattered in the ancient as in the modern world, and their distinctive places of worship and study could be found in virtually every place of commercial importance. The local congregations gave the apostles the privilege of witnessing to their faith. Acts has preserved several examples of the sermons that Paul preached. It is unlikely that these are verbatim transcripts; instead, they present Luke's conception of what the apostle ought to have said in the particular situation. That Paul and others did preach to Jews along the lines indicated by Acts is altogether probable, although the penetrating bite and intense Christ-consciousness of the letters have been mostly subdued.

In any case, the historic revelation to Israel formed the starting point, just as in the speech attributed to Stephen. The salvation which God had intended to accomplish for his chosen people, beginning with Abraham, has now been brought to fulfillment: Jesus, descended from royal David, is the promised Savior. Tragically, " those who live in Jerusalem and their rulers " did not recognize Jesus as what he really is, but asked Pilate to have him killed. Nevertheless, God raised him from the dead, thus making good on his ancient promises. " Let it be known to you therefore, brethren, that through this man forgiveness of sins is proclaimed to you, and by him every one that believes is freed from everything from which you could not be freed by the law of Moses." (Acts 13:38-39.) The sermon closes with a warning about the consequences of rejecting the One through whom God has chosen to act.

Some Jews and perhaps many of the Gentile " God-fearers "
who frequented the synagogues accepted the message and became Christians, Nazarenes, or whatever title Paul's converts
may have adopted. (Paul himself nowhere uses the term
" Christian.") The majority of the Jews did not believe,
whether at Iconium or elsewhere, as Paul sadly conceded near
the close of his career. The usual reactions seem to have been
derision and violent hostility. Again and again Paul was
beaten by resentful Jews, sometimes within the prescribed discipline of the synagogue, often in disorderly riots. Acts relates
that they often pursued him from city to city, warning their
compatriots against his blasphemous propaganda. On occasion
they indicted him before the civil authorities but, Acts reports,
with scant success. Yet Paul, despite his threat to turn to the
Gentiles, never abandoned his efforts to reach Israel " according to the flesh." The reasons for his persistence will be pres-
ently noted.

The motivations of Jewish repugnance to him and his message were of a piece with those which earlier had stirred up
Paul himself: the absurd claim that a crucified Galilean peas-
ant could possibly be God's Messiah; the further absurdity,
amounting to blasphemy, that such an impostor could do
what the hallowed law could not do; and the strong implication, if not the plain assertion, that uncircumcised Gentiles by
their faith in the Messiah might be granted a share in the
coming salvation — such a message meant the end of true religion and the adulteration of the holy nation! Add to that a
secular consideration which should perhaps be read between
the lines: all this talk about a Messiah and his imminent judgment of the entire world could only be interpreted by the
Romans as evidence of a Jewish plot against the Empire. Dispersion Jews were generally not unhappy with their lot. However fondly they might regard the land of Israel in Palestine,

they were content to enjoy the undeniable benefits of Roman rule. Nor did they desire to be identified with the senseless rebellions which flared up from time to time in Judea. Granted, as must be, that Paul had not the slightest concern with political revolution (Rom., ch. 13, was not the work of a fifth columnist!), his message may have carried overtones of sedition, not only to vigilant Romans but also to Hellenized Jews who had no feeling for the Messianic and apocalyptical strains in their professed faith. Thus, resentments, both religious and political, must have piled up against Paul in the Jewish communities that he visited.

" And Also to the Greek "

The dramatic challenge that Paul and Barnabas threw before their critics in the synagogue of Pisidian Antioch merits quotation, inasmuch as it stated the program that Paul followed in his entire career: " It was necessary that the word of God should be spoken first to you. Since you thrust it from you, and judge yourselves unworthy of eternal life, behold, we turn to the Gentiles " (Acts 13:46). Antioch of Pisidia cannot have been the first place where Paul announced his concern with Gentiles so openly — we have earlier conjectured that he worked among them from the outset. To the Galatians he claimed that God had called him for this exact purpose, " in order that I might preach him [Christ] among the Gentiles " (Gal. 1:16). Paul acknowledged that others might legitimately confine their preaching to the circumcised, but he unwaveringly insisted that he himself had been given responsibility for Greeks and barbarians: " For so the Lord has commanded us, saying, ' I have set you to be a light for the Gentiles, that you may bring salvation to the uttermost parts of the earth ' " (Acts 13:47).

By linking his vocation with the commission given to the

ideal Servant of the Lord in the Second Isaiah, Paul announced plainly his belief that Jesus the Messiah was indeed the consummation of God's redemptive purpose, a purpose that could not be restricted to Israel alone. His conception of his peculiar calling as an apostle of Jesus provides the key to an understanding of his controversies with other Jews, believers and unbelievers alike, as well as of his distinctively positive contributions to Christian thought and the expansion of the church.

In the nature of the case, Paul's appeal to Gentiles started from other premises than those which were most persuasive to Jews. Aside from the half-proselyte " God-fearers," Gentiles could be expected to know little or nothing about the traditional categories of Biblical religion. To be sure, ancient men respected all sacred books, from whatever source, so that Christian preachers were able to make effective use of those Old Testament passages which seemed to predict Jesus and his saving work. Nevertheless, the basic assumptions of the average Gentile were only minimally congenial with the distinctive elements of Israel's faith. Thus Paul had to begin with ideas comprehensible to those who listened, hoping to lead them patiently into the strange, new world of the Bible. Here, again, we must regard Luke's reports as only broadly indicative of the manner in which Paul sought to bridge the gap between a gospel organically rooted in the history and faith of Israel and the religious axioms of Gentile culture.

Two sermons recorded by Acts (chs. 14:15-17; 17:22-31) illustrate the opening gambits used by many early heralds of the good news, and Paul probably employed the pattern, if not the exact words. At Lystra he and Barnabas, having healed a lame man, were showered with divine honors by the awe-struck populace. No treatment could have more appalled a Jew, so that the apostles hastened to disclaim any divine status:

" We also are men, of like nature with you " (ch. 14:15). The affirmation of a common humanity with the Lystrans led naturally to the distinctive corollary so basic in Biblical faith: the existence of only one living God, the creator of all that is.

This theme was developed more at length in Paul's Athenian speech, where he capitalized on an altar dedicated " To an unknown god." Although we cannot be certain that Athenians actually did maintain such an altar, the thrust of more enlightened Greek philosophy and religion was in the direction of some unitary conception of deity. Uneducated persons were less monotheistically (or pantheistically) inclined, it may be, yet even to them the Jewish-Christian belief in the oneness of God could be communicated. Further, the futility of idolatry had to be exposed, and this effort formed an important part of the apostolic approach to pagans. In any case, these elementary ideas furnished a common ground of discourse, from which the Christian preacher could proceed in his attempt to make Jesus meaningful.

The speech at Lystra is so abbreviated that we can only infer the manner of transition from the argument for monotheism to the presentation of Jesus. In the Athenian sermon Jesus is abruptly introduced as the " man whom he [God] has appointed " to judge the world in righteousness. The proof of this is found in the resurrection, the fact of which is merely asserted, without corroborative evidence. This is a bare-bones summary, no more; Acts has left to the reader's imagination Paul's elaboration of the themes of threatening divine judgment and the universal human need of salvation. It can scarcely be supposed that the blunt proclamation of such a message brought immediate acceptance. The broadside against human sinfulness in Rom. 1:18-32 more accurately reflects Paul's eloquence in evangelical persuasion. In another connection Acts has, we may be sure, summed up the climactic appeal: " Be-

lieve in the Lord Jesus Christ and you will be saved." But behind the simple invitation lay abundant testimony to the grace
and power of Christ, drawn from the most intimate experience
of the apostle himself.

Once disciples had been gathered, there remained the task
of giving them instruction in the faith and of organizing them
into a group able to survive the storms and stresses of an often
antagonistic environment. The customary procedure of the
apostles is indicated by Acts: after a successful visit to Derbe,
Paul and Barnabas returned to Lystra, Iconium, and Antioch,
"strengthening the souls of the disciples, exhorting them to
continue in the faith, and saying that through many tribula-
tions we must enter the kingdom of God" (ch. 14:22). In
addition, they appointed elders in every church, the simple beginning of the elaborate hierarchical organization that domi-
nated later Christianity. Paul seems to have placed little stress
on institutional structure. In his letters he refers to various
types of service and leadership, as in I Cor. 12:4-11; Rom. 12:4-
8; and Eph. 4:11. In these passages, however, there is no hint
of formal appointment or election. The functions are per-
formed through the power and guidance of the Spirit; "there
are varieties of gifts, but the same Spirit; . . . and there are
varieties of working, but it is the same God who inspires them
all in every one" (I Cor. 12:4, 6). Acts was written at a time
when "charismatic" or Spirit-energized phenomena were less
common in the church, and when affairs were directed by regu-
larly appointed officials. Although Paul thought of "church
government" in rather more spontaneous terms, it is not unlikely that even in his groups there existed some recognized
divisions and gradations of authority. Of the nature of the
postconversion instruction given to new disciples, more must
be said in connection with our later summary of his teaching.

We have rapidly recapitulated Luke's narrative of the "first" missionary campaign of Paul and Barnabas. It matters little whether or not he set forth the course of events in their proper order. The important feature is that he has painted a vivid picture here, as also in his report of other journeys, of the manner in which the apostle penetrated virgin territory in behalf of the gospel. Every conflict, failure, and success described by Luke was repeated in town after town of Asia Minor and Greece, with changes chiefly in the names and places. The life of an apostle to the Gentiles was a ceaseless round of adventures, of dangers and disappointments, of controversy and fellowship. But it was the only life possible for a man who said, " Woe to me if I do not preach the gospel! "

CHAPTER 4 | *The Road to Rome*

THE FORK IN THE ROAD

THE success of Paul and Barnabas precipitated a struggle of crucial importance for the future of the church. Simply stated, the problem was this: Was faith in Jesus Christ sufficient for salvation, or were the requirements of Old Testament law still binding, even upon the people of the Messiah? According to Acts the question was first raised and answered when Peter baptized Cornelius and his family. It bobbed up again, nevertheless, following the mission to Cyprus and lower Galatia, where considerable numbers of Gentiles had been brought into the church. Some men from Judea came to Antioch, dogmatically teaching that "unless you are circumcised according to the custom of Moses, you cannot be saved" (Acts 15:1). These men may have been Pharisees who had joined the Nazarenes of Jerusalem (cf. ch. 15:5). Their contention was unequivocal: a Christian must also be a Jew: Gentile converts must therefore become Jewish proselytes concomitantly with their baptism and admission into the church. Such a position threw down the gage squarely before Paul, who had gone to Gentiles asking only faith (but how much he meant by that!) in God's Son, the Messiah and Lord. It brought into doubt the worth of all that he was doing in the service of his Master.

Neither Paul nor the "integrated" church at Antioch could ignore the challenge.

As in other details of the apostolic history, the respective versions of the crisis do not neatly agree. Acts relates that Paul and Barnabas sharply debated with the men from Judea, until the Antioch community appointed a delegation to lay the matter before the apostles and elders in Jerusalem. At this meeting the "liberal" view was eloquently argued by Peter, who recalled his own authorization by God to offer the gospel to Gentiles. The Holy Spirit had confirmed the rightness of this extension, and God had made "no distinction between us [Jews] and them, but cleansed their hearts by faith" (ch. 15:8-9). In a very Pauline vein, Peter asserted that not even born Jews had been able to bear the heavy yoke of the law. Why then, he asked, should Gentile disciples be burdened with it? There is now one all-embracing way of salvation, "through the grace of the Lord Jesus" (ch. 15:11). Paul and Barnabas seconded Peter's advocacy by relating "what signs and wonders God had done through them among the Gentiles" (ch. 15:12).

The prestige of Peter opened the door to an amicable settlement of the dispute. James (who appears here to be the leader of the Jerusalem church) proposed a compromise, which was embodied in an encyclical letter to be sent to Gentile believers in Antioch, Syria, and Cilicia. The Gentile Christian was to avoid any possible involvement in pagan idolatry; he was to eat only meat that had been slaughtered in the "kosher" manner; and he was to practice the rigorous sex ethic of Judaism. There was no mention of circumcision or Sabbath observance, customs that were regarded as essential by the orthodox Jew.

James's stipulations remind us of the earlier Jewish "Noachian Commands," which seem to have been applied to "Godfearers" who wished to associate with Jews in the synagogue.

In any case, James intended to formulate the ground rules according to which Christian Jews might engage in social intercourse with Gentile Christians. Acts does not make it clear that this " apostolic decree " was promulgated as the *sine qua non* of salvation for Gentiles, although conservative Jewish believers undoubtedly understood it as such. Paul supposedly accepted this middle-of-the-road solution, promising to apply it to his converts.

The more direct evidence of Paul's letters places a rather different construction on the entire episode. Galatians, ch. 2, gives the salient facts: " after fourteen years " (reckoning either from his conversion or from his " after three years " visit), in obedience to a revelation Paul, Barnabas, and Titus went to Jerusalem. Privately he explained to " those who were of repute " the message that he had been preaching among Gentiles. Some " false brethren secretly brought in " attempted to compel Titus to be circumcised, but Paul would not concede the point, and the Jerusalem leaders sustained him. The false brothers may not have been believers, but Jews hostile to the Christian movement. How they got into the conference at all is obscure.

Undaunted by opposition, Paul made a strong plea for the validity of his message and accomplishments. Although for some reason he desired the approval of the Jerusalem apostles, he plainly had no intention of altering his procedure. Somewhat defiantly he asserted that " those . . . who were of repute added nothing to me " (Gal. 2:6). The discussion was ended when James, Cephas (Peter), and John agreed that they would work among Jews (only?), while Paul and his companions were to concentrate on Gentiles. Paul made one concession, but one not involving abandonment of his principles: " only they would have us remember the poor [of Jerusalem], which very thing I was eager to do " (Gal. 2:10). He had won a victory on the main issue: the ritual laws of Judaism were not binding on Gentile believers. Or so he thought.

The issue, it turned out, was irrepressible. Sometime later Cephas visited Antioch and mingled freely with Gentiles in the church. But his rejection of segregation was short-lived; when agents of James came, he reverted to Jewish exclusiveness, "fearing the circumcision party" (Gal. 2:12). Even Barnabas reneged, being influenced by what Paul called the "insincerity" of the "rest of the Jews." Paul hit the ceiling! With biting sarcasm he defined the real issue. It involved vastly more than simply the choice of table companions. Rather, the sufficiency of Christ as Savior was at stake. Does salvation come by obedience to Jewish law and custom, *plus* belief in Christ Jesus? Or is salvation the gracious gift of God bestowed on all who have faith in Christ, quite apart from the requirements of the law? He answered his own question unequivocally: "A man is not justified by works of the law, but through faith in Jesus Christ. . . . For if justification were through the law, then Christ died to no purpose" (Gal. 2:16, 21). In the vehemence of his anger he went so far as to say that not even a Jew should observe the law, at least with the expectation that such obedience would put him right with God. The basis and guarantee of nondiscrimination is both simple and inescapable: "There is neither Jew nor Greek, there is neither slave nor free, there is neither male nor female; for you are all one in Christ Jesus" (Gal. 3:28).

Aside from the very perplexing problems of chronology that a comparison of Acts, ch. 15, and Gal., ch. 2, raises, the two passages seem to describe different conferences, different solutions — and different Pauls! The Paul of Galatians shows absolutely no awareness of any "apostolic decree" specifying technical requirements for full participation in the Christian community. If he had agreed to such limitations, the whole force of his protest at Antioch would have been negated. Although in several letters he cautioned his churches against indiscriminate association with unbelievers, he never absolutely forbade the eating of meat that came from an animal previously slaughtered in a pagan sacrifice. Neither did he restrict the Christian diet to blood-free, " kosher " meat. For the rest, he frequently attacked sexual sins and set a perfectionist, almost ascetic standard of personal chastity.

Indeed, Paul aimed to inculcate the highest ethical values of both Jewish and Greek culture. But he stoutly maintained that neither ritualistic nor moral achievements could serve as the ground or cause of salvation. Moral virtue, always imperfect in men of the present age, was seen by him as the *result* of divine grace received by human faith, the " fruit of the Spirit." No formal, external item of religious behavior could be permitted to stand prior or superior to faith in Christ. Even if it be assumed that the rules of Acts, ch. 15, were intended merely to govern social relations within the church, rather than to postulate conditions of final salvation (after the manner of many American " white " Christians, who are eager to evangelize " colored " people but not willing to share churches or schools with them), it is inconceivable that Paul could have subscribed to such rules.

It is a truism of Biblical study that every issue should be seen in its historical context. Thus, it should be kept in mind that the earliest disciples were Jewish, by birth, education, and religion. They had no intention of separating themselves from their Jewish heritage — no more than did Martin Luther expect to withdraw from the Roman Catholic Church in 1517. What we call the " Old Testament " was their only Bible; the God of Abraham, Moses, and David was the God and Father of Jesus the Messiah, and their God; the " Christ-event " was no isolated phenomenon, but the continuation and climax of what God had been doing in and for Israel all along. They were, however, convinced that the authentic people of God now included only those who accepted the Messiah: from their point of view Jews who did not accept him were apostate, no longer entitled to the blessings of the divine election. Therefore, to "convert" a Gentile and to receive him into the church was also, in a true sense, to "naturalize" him religiously into Israel. Biological descent was not the constitutive factor — as John the Baptist and Jesus had already proclaimed. Decision for or against the Messiah drew the line of division between God's Israel and the segment of mankind doomed to judgment. A Gentile could make the proper decision.

Nevertheless, two positions developed within the church. The first assumed the continuing authority of the Mosaic law — Jesus had not "come to abolish the law and the prophets . . . but to fulfil them. . . . Not an iota, not a dot, will pass from the law until all is accomplished" (Matt. 5:17-18). All had not yet been accomplished: believers awaited the return of their Messiah. So the law remained in force for his people. A second view, represented best by Paul, held identical convictions down to the point of the status of the law since Christ. Paul contended that the law had been superseded by Christ. Its regulations were no longer binding on anyone who had faith in Christ. Whatever value circumcision or any other element in the Mosaic code may once have possessed, that value was gone.

It is not to be wondered that confusion arose. To Jews in general, and not least to many who shared the faith in Jesus, Paul appeared to be offering the precious privileges of the chosen people at bargain-basement rates. It was as though a modern American judge were to confer citizenship on aliens who were not sworn to uphold the Constitution. If Paul had totally dissociated his work from the people and faith of Israel, Jews would not have pursued him so relentlessly, perhaps not at all. But because he sought to redefine both the faith and the chosen people by reference to Jesus Christ, he made himself the target of Jewish hostility, some of it emanating from within the church.

THE GOSPEL GOES WEST

The precise date of the crucial conference between Paul and the Jerusalem apostles cannot be determined. Acts leads us to think that it came relatively early in Paul's career, whereas Paul's letter places it some fourteen or seventeen years after his conversion. Unfortunately, the date of the conversion is similarly indeterminable. Scholarly conjecture has placed it as early as A.D. 30 and as late as A.D. 40. It is enough to recognize that by approximately A.D. 50 Paul had extended his missionary operations at least as far as Corinth. This extension is described by Acts within the framework of what is usually called the " second journey."

A more fruitful way of surveying the apostle's work is in terms of the geographical areas he covered. After the barely mentioned phase in Arabia he spent more than a decade in those areas of modern Syria and southeastern Turkey of which Damascus and Antioch were the natural capitals. Then he pushed progressively farther into Asia Minor, at length coming to the Aegean Sea not far from the Hellespont. Next he ventured into the mainland of Europe, traversing Greek territory from Philippi in Macedonia to the Corinthian isthmus. Finally he settled in the Roman province of Asia, now western Turkey, and used Ephesus as the base of a fruitful mission. Whatever may have been the order and direction of his travels, Paul's most substantial and enduring achievements were gained on both sides of the Aegean basin in cities relatively remote from Palestine. All his extant letters were addressed to churches of areas in which Greco-Roman culture flourished, none to the more Semitic centers of the Syro-Palestinian area. Although both the book of Acts and Paul himself regard his itinerary as Spirit-planned, he consciously aimed to concentrate his efforts on places where Christ had not previously been preached. Others followed his trail, and some sought to sabotage what he had accomplished. But Paul powerfully put his own stamp on the churches that he gathered and they preserved his unique contributions to the church universal.

"Come Over to Macedonia . . ."

After many years of collaboration, Paul and Barnabas came to a parting of ways. Acts explains the break by Paul's refusal to take John Mark on a second journey. The letter to the Galatians, on the other hand, implies that Paul would not brook the vacillating attitude of Barnabas toward Gentile disciples, and this seems closer to the fact. In any case, Paul started out again with Silas (or Silvanus), later picking up other traveling companions along the way. The party followed a snakelike path from Syrian Antioch northward through the heart of Asia Minor. Luke has preserved only a bare outline of the campaign, yet a few incidents are reported in gratifying detail and suggest the magnitude of the achievement.

Going by land, Paul revisited his churches in Syria, Cilicia, and some of the cities at which he and Barnabas had earlier touched. A puzzling note in Acts tells that he circumcised young Timothy, the son of a Greek-Jewish family. This is quite out of character for Paul, and the story can be accepted as historical only on the dubious assumption that in his eagerness to evangelize Jews, Paul was willing to adopt measures of pure expediency. The recruitment of Timothy, however, cannot be questioned, for he loyally assisted Paul throughout the arduous years in Greece and Asia. Beyond the boundaries of familiar regions some adverse circumstance was taken by Paul as divine guidance to turn to the north, rather than to more obvious opportunities in the direction of Ephesus. He headed toward Bithynia on the Black Sea, but again the Spirit intervened, guiding him to Troas, near the ruins of storied Troy. There, in a dream, a man besought him to "come over to Macedonia and help us." What lay behind the visionary experience cannot now be recovered — some chance meeting with a Macedonian, perhaps, or a secretly cherished wish to see firsthand the "glory that was Greece." Nor should it be surmised that Europe would not have been evangelized if Paul had turned back to the Orient — in all probability the Christian message in some form had already reached Rome. Nevertheless, guesses aside, Paul did enter Europe and became the greatest pioneer in the winning of the West for Christ.

The European foothold was gained at Philippi, where a hospitable businesswoman, Lydia, became the first convert. Thereafter the story in Acts moves at a rapid pace, reproducing the general pattern of experiences that had characterized the earlier mission into southern Asia Minor. In town after town Paul and his companions made their initial appeal to the resident Jewish community. Apparently Philippi included too few male Jews to form a synagogue, so the preachers found only a group of women "God-fearers" meeting for prayer by a river.

In Thessalonica, despite some modest success in the synagogue, Paul met really formidable Jewish opposition. For three weeks he was allowed to advance the Scriptural proofs that Jesus was the promised Messiah. Vehement arguments must have arisen, for unconvinced Jews dragged Paul's party before the civil magistrates. The charge was serious: "These men who have turned the world upside down have come here also . . . they are all acting against the decrees of Caesar, saying that there is another king, Jesus" (Acts 17:6 f.). This was, of course, a distortion of the Pauline gospel, and the sincerity

of those who made the charge may be questioned. Nevertheless, it was the only accusation that would be recognized by
Gentile officials. The dramatic scene before the tribunal of
Gallio at Corinth was doubtless repeated many times elsewhere. The Roman proconsul could discern no violation of imperial law in the activities of Paul: "Since it is a matter of
questions about words and names and your own law, see to it
yourselves; I refuse to be a judge of these things" (Acts 18:15).
In effect Gallio remanded Paul to the permitted discipline of
the Jewish community — a discipline that Paul did not always
escape, as he related to the Corinthians: "Five times I have
received at the hands of the Jews the forty lashes less one" (II
Cor. 11:24).

In no place, it appears, did Paul succeed in turning the synagogue into a church; everywhere the majority of his own people resisted him as a scandal to their holy religion and a threat
to their peaceful coexistence with Gentiles.

"In Danger from Gentiles . . ."

Gentiles, on the contrary, proved to be in general less hostile
and more responsive to the apostolic message. Some who listened appreciatively to Paul belonged, as did Lydia in Philippi,
to the group of wistful God-fearers on the fringe of every synagogue. Many other Gentile hearers, it is likely, had little previous acquaintance with Judaism. At Philippi a jailkeeper and
his family were baptized. In Thessalonica a great many of the
devout Greeks and not a few of the leading women were per-
suaded. In Beroea the Jewish community received Paul cordially, until Thessalonican pursuers created a disturbance, but
the word was believed by "not a few Greek women of high
standing as well as men." And so it went down the coast of
Macedonia and Achaia; in each place at least a few Gentiles
found the answer to their religious longings in the magnetic

gospel of Jesus. Although Athenians were more curious than convertible, the names of Dionysius the Areopagite and Damaris are recorded among a handful of believers won in the decaying center of classical learning.

In Corinth, above all, Paul found adequate opportunity for his energies, and he remained there for eighteen months or longer. Among the Corinthian disciples were two rulers of the synagogue, but it is certain that the real strength of the church there lay in its Gentile members. This church, despite all the anxieties that it later caused Paul, represented his outstanding achievement to that point in his mission.

Paul and his companions only planted the seed: the full crop of Christianity developed after their departure, through the efforts of nameless saints who spread the contagion of their new faith among their neighbors. We are not able to compute the numerical growth of the various churches, but vagrant hints in Paul's correspondence with the Philippians, Thessalonicans, and Corinthians show clearly that a chain reaction of evangelism followed in the apostle's wake. When the church emerged from the tunnel-like obscurity of its first century into the better-documented light of the second century, the gospel was already broadly diffused around the entire perimeter of the Mediterranean. And its astounding progress was largely forwarded by very ordinary people, of the same kind as those " not many . . . wise . . . , not many . . . powerful, not many . . . of noble birth " who were brought face to face with Christ by the preaching of Paul. Even the apparent failures of Paul and other first-generation apostles were brought to fruition among the Gentiles by simple believers who both preached and lived their faith in the routine affairs of every day. Acts does little more than to hint at the means by which the church moved irresistibly through the world. Yet Luke sensibly perceived that a Paul was required to set the force in motion, and he has sketched unforgettable vignettes of the manner in which it all began.

"ALL . . . ASIA HEARD . . ."

Regrettably, Acts barely summarizes the exciting year and a half or two years that Paul spent in Corinth. From his letters to that lusty church we infer that his faith and courage were constantly put to the test. Luke recalled chiefly the conflicts with hostile Jews, probably because Paul's exoneration before Gallio provided a favorable precedent in Roman law. Gallio, incidentally, is of considerable importance to church history, inasmuch as his term of office can be dated approximately within the years A.D. 51–53, and this is the first reliable clue to the Pauline chronology. Aside from the trial, Acts casually records that Paul became acquainted with two Jewish tentmakers, Priscilla and Aquila, who had come to Corinth as refugees from Rome. A repressive decree against the Jewish community in Rome had been issued by the emperor Claudius, apparently prompted by agitation about Messianic claims in behalf of Jesus. Paul and this couple plied their common trade together, and they continued to assist him when he went to Ephesus.

Paul at length and somewhat reluctantly left Corinth, in order to blaze new trails in the populous regions of the Roman province of Asia. Acts has it that he took a peculiar vow at the Corinthian port of Cenchreae, going as far as to cut his hair in ritualistic fashion. This seems very unlike the " law-free " Paul of the letters, but his actual behavior may often have been more flexible in regard to Jewish custom than his polemical writings indicate. Stopping briefly at Ephesus, he promised some Jews in the synagogue that he would return after a trip to Judea and Syria. Few precise details of this journey are known — perhaps it represents a jumbled recollection of the conference visit elsewhere described in Acts, ch. 15. He is supposed also to have made a tour of inspection through Galatia and Phrygia en route to his main target in Asia.

Meanwhile, Priscilla and Aquila lingered in Ephesus, witnessing to the Way in the synagogue. There they encountered one of the enigmatic yet influential characters of New Testament times, Apollos from Alexandria. Although he was teaching "the things concerning Jesus" from the point of view of the Pauline party, his faith was incomplete — he "knew only the baptism of John." Apollos was not alone in this defect: Paul subsequently met twelve other "disciples" who had received John's baptism and had not even heard about the gift of the Holy Spirit.

The two episodes bristle with difficulties. They suggest at least the following possibilities: First, the influence of John the Baptist was still strong in some Jewish quarters, and the relation of Jesus to John's message of judgment and repentance was by no means clearly defined; secondly, not all followers of the "Way" (a Lucan term for Christianity) practiced either baptism in the name of Jesus or the Pentecostal type of religious behavior. The fact is, of course, that as late as two decades after Jesus the lines between Judaism as such, the sectarian movement of John, and the Christian "Way" were not sharply drawn in all particulars of belief and practice.

Acts does less than full justice to the eventful years during which Paul made Ephesus his headquarters. He preached for three months in the synagogue; being driven out (as always!), he rented a lecture hall which was also used by a Greek philosopher or rhetorician; he won a routine victory over some itinerant Jewish exorcists; there was a spectacular uprising of silversmiths against the Christian group, but Paul escaped unscathed. Paul's letters, on the other hand, disclose that these years were among the busiest of his career. It was a time of strenuous evangelization, not alone within Ephesus, but throughout the entire area, reaching as far as Laodicea, Colossae, and Hierapolis. Quarrels racked the Corinthian church, calling forth written remonstrances from Paul, as well as some mediating visits by him and Timothy. There is reason to think that the historic conference with the Jerusalem apostles occurred either just before or during this period, and that the letter to the Galatians was written from Ephesus. Paul possibly served a prison term there, and many scholars assign the prison letters — Philemon, Philippians, and Colossians — to that unhappy interlude. From Ephesus, too, Paul doubtless began his cherished collection from Gentile Christians for impoverished believers in Jerusalem. From every point of view, the turbulence of the Ephesian ministry brought to full maturity the creative powers of Paul as an interpreter of Christ and an architect of the growing church.

THE LAST PILGRIMAGE

More than fear of the silversmiths prompted Paul to leave Ephesus. The dissensions at Corinth were not yet resolved, and he felt that his presence there might repair the broken unity of the church. Uppermost in his thoughts was the collection for Jerusalem, the project of reconciliation between Jewish and Gentile believers which he had been encouraging through his letters and personal emissaries. Finally, as he wrote to the Roman Christians, he no longer saw " room for work in these regions " of the Aegean, and he proposed to carry the gospel to the westernmost boundary of civilization in Spain. Accordingly, Paul turned toward Macedonia and Greece. It was not a carefree journey: " When we came into Macedonia, our bodies had no rest but we were afflicted at every turn " (II Cor. 7:5). What these afflictions were, we do not know. Some encouragement was gained from news that the Corinthian situation had improved, a development that is reflected in the optimistic letter now found in II Cor., chs. 1-9. Proceeding into Greece, he remained for several months, probably at Corinth. From there he wrote to the Roman church, announcing his plan to visit it after the collection had been delivered in Jerusalem. A Jewish plot in Corinth made it advisable for him to head toward Syria by way of Philippi. There he observed the Passover, an indication that he had not broken completely with Jewish customs.

The ensuing voyage southward along the coast of Asia Minor and Syria reminds us of the journey Jesus made when " he set his face to go to Jerusalem " (Luke 9:51). Despite the apostle's joy over the success of the collection, a mood of imminent tragedy pervades the story in Acts. At Miletus he made an impassioned farewell speech to elders from Ephesus, in which he reviewed his past work and speculated somberly about the fate awaiting him in Jerusalem. Disciples in Tyre warned him — " through the Spirit " — not to continue the journey; at Caesarea the mysterious prophet Agabus (cf. Acts 11:28) accurately predicted Paul's coming arrest. But nothing could deter him: " For I am ready not only to be imprisoned but even to die at Jerusalem for the name of the Lord Jesus " (Acts 21:13). At long last he reached his destination and was received cordially by the disciples.

Acts is strangely silent about the reception of the Gentile contribution. This generous gesture, on which Paul had staked so much, is overshadowed by the story of his arrest. Jewish hostility toward the champion of the Gentiles had not yet spent itself. The Jerusalem apostles urged Paul to demonstrate publicly to the " thousands . . . among the Jews of those who have believed " that he had not really taught Dispersion Jews to reject the law or, for that matter, repudiated it in his own manner of living. In compliance with this advice, Paul agreed to sponsor four men who were performing certain vows. This was his undoing: some Asian Jews accused him of bringing Greeks into the forbidden precincts of the Temple, an offense punishable by death. A lynch mob quickly gathered, and Paul's life hung in balance. Only the intervention of the Roman garrison saved him, and he was put under protective arrest. Thus Paul passed into Roman custody, from which he probably never emerged as a free man.

It is not necessary here to rehearse the several interrogations of Paul before the Sanhedrin, the procurators Felix and Festus, and King Herod Agrippa II. These questionings gave him the occasion of proclaiming the mighty acts of God in Christ under the most prominent circumstances. His accusers tried to substantiate the charge that Paul had committed a capital offense against Jewish law and should be remanded to the jurisdiction of the Sanhedrin. Paul flatly denied this, arguing that he was being persecuted because he, a Pharisee, taught the Pharisaic doctrine of the resurrection from the dead. This rebuttal — which shifted the case from legal to theological grounds — did not squarely meet the indictment but it did provoke dissension within the Sanhedrin, since some Pharisees leaped to Paul's defense.

The Roman governors were caught in the middle, utterly baffled by theological subtleties of a religion always incomprehensible to hardheaded administrators. They were torn between two inclinations: on the one side, neither Felix nor Festus could discover any clear violation of Roman law; on the other, both hesitated to release a potential revolutionist. Their dilemma was finally resolved when Paul, as a Roman citizen, impatiently exercised his right of appeal to the Emperor. Thereby the procurators were relieved of immediate responsibility, and Paul was removed from the explosive situation in Judea. To the apostle, his appeal brought both a reprieve from Jewish conspiracies and the coveted opportunity of penetrating the very center of the civilized world with his gospel.

THE ROAD TO ROME AND . . . ?

The classic story of the voyage is told in the first person plural — one of the " we " sections which tradition has credited to Luke's travel diary — and preserves authentic information on ancient navigation. Although he was a prisoner, Paul cautioned the ship's captain against sailing beyond Fair Havens on Crete, until the winter storms should subside. His warnings were ignored, with the result that the ship was badly crippled by violent gales. Having been promised in a vision that he would yet " stand before Caesar," Paul was able to lift the morale of all on board, even preventing the crew from abandoning the ship and its human cargo. When the drifting vessel finally ran aground on Malta, evident signs of divine favor toward Paul induced suspicious natives to assist the beleaguered company. He resisted a viper's bite on his own arm and went on to perform miraculous cures of many sick inhabitants. No misadventure could thwart the apostle's destined course, and the captives at last reached the shores of southern Italy.

The weary prisoner and his companions (who seemingly were not under arrest) were cordially received by " brethren " at Puteoli and elsewhere along the Appian Way to Rome. Paul's reputation, enhanced no doubt by his letter to the Romans, had excited interest in the controversial champion of Gentile believers. After he had become established in private quarters, however, he turned his attention to the Jewish community as a whole. Since he was not free to attend synagogue services, Paul summoned its local leaders to consult with him. As so often before, he stoutly maintained the legitimacy of his work, even within the Judaistic frame of reference: he had done nothing against "the people or the customs of our fathers." His sole "crime" was his revealed certainty that the "hope of Israel" had been fulfilled in Jesus, and he adduced proof from both the Law and the Prophets of the Hebrew Bible.

The invited leaders professed to have received no report on Paul from official circles in Jerusalem. They were eager, indeed, to learn more about "this sect" that everywhere was a cause of dispute. The request is curious, inasmuch as some kind of Christian group had existed in Rome for at least a decade before Paul arrived there. No available evidence names the person who first preached the gospel there, yet there can be no question that a church had already been formed. The episode in Acts may reflect Luke's implied view that the only really valid version of Christian faith was the message preached by Paul. Nevertheless, the argument of Paul's letter, written some two or three years earlier, suggests that both Jews and Gentiles were included in the number of Roman believers.

Not without precedent, Paul's appeal to his Jewish compatriots met indifferent response. Accordingly, after the example set by Jesus (Mark 4:12), he applied to them Isaiah's verdict upon the faithless people of eighth-century Judah: "You shall indeed hear but never understand, and you shall indeed see but never perceive" (Acts 28:26; cf. Isa. 6:9). Turning sadly from his obdurate fellow Jews, Paul addressed himself once again to Gentiles: "They will listen." Thus he continued for two years, "preaching the kingdom of God and teaching about the Lord Jesus Christ quite openly and unhindered" (Acts 28:31). The die was cast; Israel "according to the flesh" had forfeited its historical pre-eminence in God's purpose; a New Israel "according to the Spirit" was being gathered to receive the promise. On this note Acts rings down the curtain on Paul.

CHAPTER 5 | *The Gospel in the Letters*

T HE story of Paul's missionary adventures is both inspiring
and fascinating. Yet that story is important chiefly because it
provides the setting for something of greater importance —
Paul's message about Jesus Christ. For this message we must
turn to the letters that Paul wrote, which open windows into
his mind and heart. Few men of antiquity may be so inti-
mately known to us. In contrast to the formal, studied " epistles " of most other notable figures in ancient history, the letters of Paul reflect his spontaneous " conversations " with his
Christian friends. He sent letters only when he could not make
personal visits. Dictating his words to trusted companions who
could scarcely keep pace, the apostle poured out his thoughts
in mixed thanksgiving, instruction, and exhortation. Truly
were those letters " weighty and strong " (II Cor. 10:10).

Paul may not be ignored or lightly dismissed. On the contrary, there is no sufficient understanding of the Christian faith
apart from the major insights of this ancient, yet timeless, interpreter of the gospel. And fortunately, despite all obscurities,
the essential faith of the man shines through his letters to every generation. The " heart of the matter " of salvation is there

— the clear proclamation that "God shows his love for us in that while we were yet sinners Christ died for us. . . . Since we are justified by faith, we have peace with God through our Lord Jesus Christ. . . . For as in Adam all die, so also in Christ shall all be made alive." While the full implications of this proclamation may not be instantly evident, it stands as the core of the Christian proclamation, so far as the faith can be put into words at all. Granting every obvious difference between the first century and the twentieth, the spiritual and ethical problems of human existence continue much the same in all ages, so that Paul speaks still to the " condition " of sinful but sensitive men.

Although no reconstruction of the order in which Paul wrote his letters can be regarded as incontestably reliable, it is helpful to read them in some sequence such as that outlined in Chapter 1. Thus, the proper starting place is the Thessalonian correspondence, sent from Corinth not later than A.D. 51. Since the problems of the predominantly Gentile Corinthian church resemble those encountered at Thessalonica, especially on the ethical side, the several letters to Corinth should be considered next. " Several," we say, because the present two letters have been formed from at least four originally separate communications: (1) II Cor. 6:11 to 7:2; (2) I Corinthians; (3) II Cor., chs. 10 to 13; (4) II Cor., chs. 1 to 9. Most of these seem to have been written during the fateful years in Ephesus, and they show us how anxiously Paul supervised the welfare of those who had come to know Christ through his preaching.

The letter to the Galatians has long been in dispute among scholars, many of whom have thought it to be the earliest of Paul's writings. Misled by Acts, ch. 15, some have felt that the controversy over Christian adherence to the Jewish law was settled quite early in Paul's career, so that the argument of Galatians would have been unnecessary in the later stages of his work. The more probable view is that such an argument had to be made again and again, to the very end of the apostle's life. Consequently, Galatians may be studied at almost any point in his career, since it reflects Paul's impassioned attempt to deal with the first major distortion of the gospel — the recurring substitution of human merit for God's grace as the ground of salvation. Similarly, the letter to the Romans need not be tied too closely to any particular stage of Paul's activity. This letter is more in the style of a " book," as we normally use that word. It was written as he made the last, tragic journey to Jerusalem and was intended to create a favorable climate for his projected visit to the imperial capital. In content it is virtually an extended commentary on Galatians — only in these two letters is the theme of " justification by faith " developed systematically. For many readers, Romans is the crown of the Pauline writings because it gives the most logical and eloquent statement of his distinctive message.

Colossians, Philippians, and Philemon came from some imprisonment served by Paul, perhaps during the two years in Rome, but certainly in a fairly late period of his life. Ephesians, likewise, claims an origin in prison. Whether or not Paul wrote it remains one of the unsolved mysteries of scholarly speculation. Even if he did not, its language and thought are heavily dependent upon letters that he unquestionably wrote, notably Colossians. In any event, the imprisonment letters manifest great concern with adulterations of the gospel by alien theologies seeping in from the Gentile world. On the positive side, they contain the most exalted conceptions of Christ as " the image of the invisible God," and of the church as his body.

The Pastoral Epistles — I and II Timothy, and Titus — are not regarded as authentically " Pauline " by the majority of modern Protestant scholars. It is thought that some fragments of otherwise unknown letters by Paul may be imbedded in them, particularly in II Timothy, and they are useful to introduce us to the circumstances within which Paul and other early Christian leaders worked. In the series of which this volume is a part, Professor Beker's *The Church Faces the World,* Chapter 2, gives a sympathetic account of the Pastorals.

"ACCORDING TO MY GOSPEL . . ."

There was a gospel before Paul — more than one, perhaps: the gospel of the Palestinian-Jewish Messianists, and the gospel of the Hellenistic church in which Paul himself first heard about Jesus. But when God "was pleased to reveal his Son" to the Tarsian persecutor, the conversion produced a creatively fresh interpretation of the meaning of Christ. Paul did not, indeed, consider himself an innovator: "I delivered to you," he reminded the Corinthians, "as of first importance *what I also received,* that Christ died for our sins in accordance with the scriptures, that he was buried, that he was raised on the third day . . . , and that he appeared . . ." (I Cor. 15:3 ff.). He acknowledged continuity and his indebtedness to those who were in Christ before him. But he was conscious, also, of advance in his own version of the salvation message beyond anything that previous believers had grasped. No outline or bare summary can convey the richness and profundity of those insights — nothing less than immersion in all the letters can do that. We should, however, identify the controlling themes of Paul's thought, themes that run through everything he wrote.

THE HUMAN PREDICAMENT

The Hebrew Scriptures and the continuing tradition of Judaism formed the subsoil of Paul's religious thought. Although he repudiated much of that inheritance, he nevertheless assumed the basic categories of Biblical thought. And the Old

Testament presented the religious problem in a simple yet comprehensive framework: the world had a beginning; it has a meaningful history; it will have an end, at least an end to its present tragic course. The key to all is God! God created, God controls history, God will ultimately bring the end. History, for all its evils and frustrations, is the medium of a salvation that God proposes to accomplish. This was the constant theme of the Old Testament prophets; it was the assumption upon which Paul based his total interpretation of Christ.

Salvation is required, indeed. For the created universe somehow went wrong and is chronically estranged from the Creator. Here Paul has recourse to the myth of fallen Adam, but Adam as the type and representative of all mankind — " in Adam all die " (I Cor. 15:22). Elsewhere he makes much of the " principalities and powers," demonic elements almost personal in nature, which share man's alienation from God, perhaps even make man the helpless tool of their rebellious intentions. The work of salvation cannot, in any case, be completed until the forces of supernatural evil are subjugated.

But it is man who stands at the center of God's concern — creation was subjected to futility and " waits with eager longing for the revealing of the sons of God " (Rom. 8:18 f.). Whatever the order of priority, it is human sin, not natural imperfection, that sets the problem of redemptive history. God created man " good," capable of harmonious relationship with his Creator. Disobedience changed that: all the posterity of Adam are at odds with him who made them for himself. Paul offered no consistent explanation of why and how this came about. He saw the human person as an organic unity of " flesh " and " mind " or " spirit." Although the flesh is man's point of susceptibility to sin, it is not evil in itself, nor is mind intrinsically good.

The Pauline psychology is quite ambiguous, but this much

is evident: the primary fact about every human person is that he *is* a sinner, not only in respect to particular concrete infractions of divine law, but more seriously in his very being, his congenital disposition of rebellion against God. We should note that Paul is so haunted by the terrible reality of sin that he virtually objectifies it as a malignancy independent of the will of man, a cancer which renders the self morbidly ill and impotent to accomplish even relative good. Still, the thrust of his preaching was to the human will, and we can infer that he regarded the perversion of man's desires and intentions as being crucial in the human predicament.

The good God can do no other, initially, than condemn the sinner. The inescapable consequence of sin is God's wrath. And the penalty inflicted by wrath is death. In Paul's vocabulary, " the wages of sin is death " (Rom. 6:23), the latter being considered both as the natural termination of physical life and as a state of utter spiritual separation from God. Sinful man is now thus estranged; left to himself he can only anticipate the bleak nothingness of total personal annihilation. Paul never spelled out the details of final condemnation; his first readers no doubt understood fully what he meant, and his reiteration of the theme sufficed to claim their attention for his central message of salvation.

But God, according to Paul, has never been indifferent to the apparently hopeless predicament of man. On the contrary, " what can be known about God is plain " to all men, " because God has shown it to them " (Rom. 1:19). Unfortunately, the generality of mankind has persistently rejected this revelation: " although they knew God they did not honor him as God . . . but they became futile in their thinking and their senseless minds were darkened " (ch. 1:21). In his mercy and as an expression of his righteousness, God long ago took steps to rescue humanity from the stalemate to which sin had brought it. These steps constitute the substance of God's dealings with Israel before Christ. Paul raised no questions about the anomaly of the " election " of a tiny, obscure nation as the divine strategy of salvation. A devout Jew, he took the Biblical history for granted and sought to extract its significant meanings. He found two crucial moments in that sacred past. The first was the covenant of promise to Abraham. This represents God's real intention toward man, for in it the basis of a favorable relationship was God's gracious offer of salvation, to which Abraham responded by faith and faith alone. In Romans and Galatians, particularly, Paul hammered away at Abraham's call as the proper analogy of the possibility opened up by Christ.

The stubborn facts of Israelite history, however, forced another stage of the divine initiative upon Paul's consideration. This was the Mosaic covenant at Sinai, in which the Torah was delivered to the chosen people. Here Paul, as we have earlier seen, diverged most seriously from the main stream of Judaism. To the orthodox Jew, the law was Judaism, and Judaism was the law. In the law God had set forth the explicit conditions on which a right relationship with himself could be achieved. To attack it in any manner was to threaten the very foundations of Jewish existence. Not even Paul could deny its divine origin: it was " holy and just and good " (Rom. 7:12). Yet, he contended, it had not been and could not be a positive means of salvation. History and human experience showed that clearly enough. (Rom., chs. 2, 3, and *passim*). The law defined sin in specific terms and subtly provoked men to commit transgressions. At best it could be regarded as a measure of expediency to promote order in a chaotic world, or as a device for unmasking the imperfections and helplessness of even its most conscientious observers. In so far, it could be honored as a " custodian until Christ came " (Gal. 3:24).

But it lacked dynamic power to change men at the core of their being; it could not rectify the objective results of sin.

Paul said, in effect, that no form of human " religion " could heal the rupture between man and God: the best and most that any man can do is never good enough; God can be neither coerced nor bribed; the " life " of salvation (as opposed to the " death " of condemnation) is not a reward but a *gift* to those who receive it by *faith*.

" THE RIGHTEOUSNESS OF GOD IS REVEALED . . ."

The crucial question, then, turns on the means by which God has determined to fulfill his purpose of redemption. Paul's answer is unequivocal: through Christ, and Christ alone. The man Christ Jesus provides the only way to salvation. God was " in Christ " reconciling the sinful world to himself; through him men can be " justified by faith " and enjoy peace with God. This is all very familiar and on the surface quite simple.

In fact, it is not simple at all, and Paul resorted to a wide variety of metaphors and analogies in his attempt to explain *why* the mediation of Christ is necessary and *how* it accomplishes the desired result. Unfortunately, no single passage of the letters develops a full-blown " Christology." Everything Paul wrote was focused on the " person and work " of Christ, and no brief summary can capture the richness of his views. A few observations must suffice. Paul knew about the Palestinian ministry of the man Jesus, although he made only oblique references to any details of that life. The one " historical " event that loomed above all else was the crucifixion: quite single-mindedly Paul laid exclusive stress on " Jesus Christ and him crucified " (I Cor. 2:2). He saw the cross, however, as vastly more than a miscarriage of Jewish or Roman justice. It was the watershed of salvation-history; the cross and the resurrection together constitute the objective keystones in the structure of God's redemptive plan. Both exhibit Jesus as the "power and wisdom of God," as God's Son, the very image of the invisible God.

Paul came as close as human language permits to an identification of Christ *as* God, and his words give ample support to the Trinitarian definitions of a later period. But he never wholly lost sight of the human Jesus, who in his resurrection, indeed, emerged as the first-born of many brothers (Rom. 8:29). Without bothering to analyze either the physiology or the psychology of the incarnation, Paul acknowledged Christ as both human and divine, mysteriously yet organically related to man and God. Because he was what he was, Christ was uniquely qualified to accomplish salvation.

In assaying Paul's thought we must keep in mind both the objective and the subjective aspects of Christ's work. The latter have to do with the faith-response of the individual believer — all that Paul implied by the present life in Christ. But there is that in the Christ-event which is quite independent initially of the believing faith of any individual. In the past (although everything that Paul affirms about Christ has simultaneously past, present, and future reference) the death of Jesus accomplished definite results.

Here we encounter a world of ideas that is all too strange to us. In Paul's opinion, God could not simply forgive man with a casual word and let it go at that. The righteous character of God — his uncompromising moral self-consistency — demands that sin be justly requited. In some manner the death of Christ satisfied the demand of eternal justice — he took on himself the appropriate punishment for universal sin. Or, in another way of thinking, Paul had recourse to the sacrificial system of ancient Judaism (and of all ancient religions), with its ideas of atonement and expiation of sin through bloody offerings on the altar. No modern rationalizations can make such ideas either intelligible or palatable, yet they are imbedded firmly in Paul's theology. Again, he spoke as though Christ had paid a ransom or taken other action whereby sinful man might gain release from slavery or imprisonment. The recipient of such payment is not clear: is it God or the demonic powers? These problems can be illuminated (never fully solved!) only by careful study. But one major point we can and must recognize: Paul did not locate the saving significance of Christ primarily in any sublime, timeless truths that Jesus enunciated. No — God in Christ *did* something that *had* to be done if the rehabilitation and reconciliation of sinners were to be anything more than a pious dream.

A similar objectivity characterizes Paul's view of the end. Christ will *do* something: he will come, and those who belong to him will come with him; he will deliver " the kingdom to God the Father after destroying every rule and every authority and power." Then, " when all things are subjected to him . . . the Son himself will also be subjected to him who put all things under him, that God may be everything to every one " (I Cor. 15:24, 28). The drama which had a beginning in creation and has spun out its tragic action through history is to have a final act, a consummation which shades over into the Kingdom of God. Sin and its corollary, death, are to be destroyed; all that remains then will be " life," which means existence in perfect harmony with God. This is the final achievement of the death and resurrection of Christ. Paul drew no pictures of heaven or hell; he scrupulously avoided the fantasies of apocalypticism. He did not speculate further on the fate of those who had rejected the proffered reconciliation with God. There is even a hint that none will be ultimately lost. But, again, the end is presented in quite objective terms — it is no purely " inner " and " spiritual " absorption of the individual soul into the Absolute. Rather, the diseased creation shall be made well again, the humanity that had lost its birthright in Adam shall find its true destiny in Christ: " for as in Adam all die, so also in Christ shall all be made alive " (I Cor. 15:22). The entire creation — and pre-eminently man — will be restored to the state that God had intended it to be in from the outset.

" BY GRACE YOU HAVE BEEN SAVED THROUGH FAITH . . ."

Between the poles of creation and consummation lies the existence that men now live " in the flesh." Here we are confronted by what may be called the subjective work of Christ, in the sense that it impinges on particular men as they are. We may imagine that the query of the Philippian jailer was often posed to Paul: " What must *I* do to be saved? " Every letter that Paul wrote was in the main an answer to that question. However persuasively he might convince men of their sinful helplessness and proclaim the grand outline of salvation-history, it was obviously never easy to show them how they could immediately share in the great redemption. This must surely have been the case for those Gentile converts who lacked the Jewish sense of belonging to a chosen people in covenant relation with God. In the heterogeneity of Greco-Roman civilization, the individual felt very much alone, and he was concerned to know how any scheme of salvation applied directly to him.

Paul's all-inclusive response was to the point: faith in Christ. Christ is not merely a crucified and resurrected Messiah temporarily retired into heaven before he hurtles back to earth to inaugurate the end; he is the living Lord of life, with whom personal and constant fellowship is available. Through him God *now* offers his grace to us; the means by which we grasp God's grace is faith. The verb that expresses the faith-response is literally " believe," but a great deal more is involved in it than the usual meaning of assent with the mind. At bottom, of course, to believe is to accept the gospel assertions as true. It implies, further, an assurance that God will fulfill his promise of salvation, that the cosmic redemption proclaimed in the apostolic message will really be completed.

But faith is something still more intimate and animating than a conviction about the truth of religious propositions. It means a self-abandonment to the God who acts in Jesus Christ; for Paul himself it meant a mystical union with the living Christ, a union so intensely felt that Paul could say, "It is no longer I who live, but Christ who lives in me; . . . the life I now live in the flesh I live by faith in the Son of God, who loved me and gave himself for me" (Gal. 2:20). The surrender of faith must be complete: there is no room for self-propelled efforts to earn merit with God. In the cross God has shown his willingness to do for man what man cannot do for himself; in the living Christ the miracle of the new creation begins and continues.

In faith the whole drama of salvation comes alive for the believer. What Christ objectively achieves becomes an intimate personal possession. The experience of reconciliation with God is ineffable in itself, but Paul ran the gamut of metaphors in his endeavor to communicate its reality. He chose various familiar situations of human pardon and release and used them as pointers toward God's gracious action in Christ. Thus he likened the predicament of the sinner to the plight of a criminal brought before a judge. The only possible plea is "guilty," and the only reasonable sentence is death. Yet the judge, out of sheer love, pronounces the felon innocent and proceeds to treat him as though he really were a decent citizen. All that the guilty man can do is to trust the judge and humbly receive the verdict given. It is in this manner, said Paul, that God "justifies him who has faith in Jesus" (Rom. 3:26).

When a man responds by faith it is *as if* he were a criminal pardoned, a slave ransomed and bought back into freedom, an orphan adopted into a family. Or it is as if one were made the beneficiary of an all-atoning sacrifice for sin — or, even, as if a dead man were raised to live again. The " as if," however, is not the whole story: the hypothesis points to a fulfillment in the final consummation. Those who are now pronounced acquitted on the basis of their faith shall become actually righteous in the image of Christ; they shall grow to " the measure of the stature of the fullness of Christ " and be united to God in perfect peace. The believer is saved now, but he is also yet to be saved. He makes no grandiose claims about himself; rather he yields himself in faith and hope to God: " Not that I have already obtained this or am already perfect; but I press on to make it my own, because Christ Jesus has made me his own " (Phil. 3:12).

Out of faith comes, too, the daily life of the Christian. Some have thought it inconsistent in Paul that he placed so much stress on ethical living. How paradoxical that the one who most sharply attacked the " works of the law " should have filled every letter with demands for the most strenuous moral effort. But no inconsistency is involved, since Paul viewed ethical achievement as the result, not the cause, of a right relationship with God through Christ. The accompaniment of faith is the " gift of the Spirit." Indeed, Paul virtually equated Christ and the Spirit of God. The believer is " in Christ " and lives henceforth by the Spirit, no longer under control of the flesh. The victory of Christ over sin is repeated in the believer, who now receives power to obey God as he could never do apart from faith. The pattern of the Christian life becomes " faith working through love "; its specific virtues are the " fruit of the Spirit . . . love, joy, peace, patience, kindness, goodness, faithfulness, gentleness, self-control; against such there is no law " (Gal.

5:22 f.). Paul never expected himself or others to attain absolute perfection in the present age. He knew that human faith is never quite complete, and the pull of the flesh remains strong. Yet he did not hesitate to lay a rigorous ethical ideal before his readers, exhorting them to " earnestly desire the higher gifts " of the Spirit, the greatest of which is love.

Epilogue

What finally happened to the greatest apostle? Was he acquitted and released? Was he executed after two years? Did he make his planned trip to Spain? Why did Luke end his book so inconclusively? Did he intend to write a third volume on the rise of Christianity? Numerous questions occur to modern readers, accustomed to abundant and precise information about famous persons. The New Testament and other ancient Christian writings do not satisfy our curiosity. Indeed, it appears that little attention was given to Paul during the two decades after his death, and Acts was perhaps in part an effort to revive his influence. Outside this book and the collected letters, only a few elusive hints concerning his fate remain from early literature. This is true, as well, of all other heroes of the apostolic age. A widely accepted tradition affirmed that Paul made further journeys to west and east; another identified the exact spot of his martyrdom under Nero outside the walls of Rome. These were pious rumors at best; the careful historian stakes little more than probability upon them.

It should be repeated that Acts was not published as a biography of Paul. Luke aimed, rather, to show how the gospel was preached and accepted from Jerusalem to Rome. In one sense he emphasized places more than persons. Once the good news had reached Rome, the story ends, its purpose accomplished. A subsidiary purpose, to be sure, was the proof of Christianity's legal status in the Empire. If Paul was actually acquitted, that fact would have added great cogency to Luke's plea. On the contrary, the conviction and execution of the apostle would have adversely affected the case so carefully assembled. The latter consideration may more adequately explain Luke's final abruptness. Speculate as we will, the important matter to Luke was what God had done through Paul, not the latter's acquittal or conviction before a fallible Roman court.

A great deal depends on the weight given to the Pastoral Epistles — I and II Timothy, and Titus. If in their extant form they represent whole letters written by Paul himself, then it must be concluded that he survived to travel again. These letters give evidence of visits to Ephesus, Troas, Macedonia, Crete, and perhaps Nicopolis. Many modern scholars believe that Paul wrote only some fragments now included in the Pastorals, and these excerpts could well have come from his career prior to the Roman imprisonment. No incontrovertible decision about the facts is possible. However, the entire tone of the narrative in Acts, from the revisiting of the Macedonian and Achaian churches to the arrival at Rome, points toward a destiny similar to the suffering of Paul's Lord on the cross. Foreboding and resignation pervade the farewell address to the Ephesian elders; each restraining prophecy along the route to Jerusalem augurs the apostle's imminent condemnation. We cannot escape the impression that Luke knew that Paul did *not* win acquittal before Caesar. The details of the tragic — and yet, by the paradox of God's ways, triumphant — end were not recorded for reasons best known to the author.

We need not doubt the old tradition that Paul, in whatever calendar year, was executed by the Roman government. But on what charge? Surely not for breach of Jewish law, since this law would have been operative in capital cases only in Judea. The effective charge must have been sedition, the fomenting of revolt against the Empire. It was an absurd charge, as Luke knew and we know. Yet it may not have seemed so foolish to a jittery dictatorship. Even as Pilate did not understand Jesus' disavowal of pretensions to a kingdom in this world, so Felix, Festus, and their sort could not grasp the transcendent reference of Paul's message. He proclaimed a hope and a Kingdom, a Messiah King who would come in judgment over the world, and an already beginning victory " through our Lord Jesus Christ." A Nero, who thought of himself also as " Lord," with connotations both secular and religious, could not afford to permit a rival. We may guess, then, that Roman bureaucrats took the safe course. Paul literally " died with Christ . . . in a death like his," yet confident that he would " certainly be united with him in a resurrection like his."